THE TRANSFORMATION OF THE SOUL

By Julian Hamer

© All rights reserved. No part of this publication may be reproduced without the prior permission of the author.
First published 2014
Revised by the author, 2022

Dedicated to my beautiful wife Ellen

THE TRANSFORMATION OF THE SOUL
From Self-Centeredness to Sovereign Autonomy

By Julian Hamer

Contents

1. Immediate Cognition p1
2. The Necessity of Soul Transformation p7
3. The Human, Singular Significance p19
4. Openhearted Sincerity p25
5. The Supernal Presence p33
6. Immediate Cognitive Engagement p39
7. Materialistic Western Philosophy p45
8. Materialism and Substance p55
9. The Tenor of Authenticity p63
10. Conventional Cognition p71
11. The Corporeal Faculties p81
12. The Intellectual Approach p87
13. Egocentricity and Defensiveness p91
14. Dimensionality p99
15. Transformation p103
16. Sincerity p109
17. Immediacy p115
18. Active Participation p121
19. Human Destiny p125
20. Soul Metamorphosis p131

Books by the same author p135

1. Immediate Cognition

The profundity of a phenomenon resides intangibly as the particular quality of the intrinsic expression of its existence. When we engage circumstances straightforwardly, and entirely without partiality, we discover the way things are not merely superficially, but inherently. Thereby, we find that the qualitative significance of something is only implied by the physical appearance, and quality does not otherwise possess material existence. Yet, it is the physically elusive, characteristic nature of things that is the most meaningful proportion.

The efficacy of the practice of immediate cognition described above may be readily illustrated through a careful examination of the usual approach that we use to discern the non-physical significance of something that we already know exists without doubt. Through direct engagement without presupposition, we recognize that, while an object has obvious physical properties, the blatant characteristics alone fail to describe adequately the more profound distinction that we otherwise appreciate. Consequently, we recognize that, through the exclusively material view, intrinsic significance remains overlooked, and the phenomenon appears from a shallow approach to lack substantial connotation. Accordingly, if we conclude that the superficial physical appearance alone is the entire significance of the existence of a thing, overlooking the characteristic nature not only robs phenomena of dimensionality, but instills in the viewer a misleading and desolate perception of life.

An example of the shallowness of an exclusively

physical depiction of phenomena may be found through the examination of the popular scientific classification of daylight. A precise physical analysis of natural light is elusive because its particular distinction can only be portrayed marginally in quantifiable terms because it is non-material. Consequently, if we were to examine exhaustively the physical evidence regarding spectrum color, try as we might, the true identity and the characteristic nature of red or blue would remain elusive. This is because solely concrete properties are negligible in terms of light, and science must fall back upon hypotheses in order to explain phenomena that are without direct physical existences, and that can be evaluated only by their effect. And like it or not, ultimately, hypotheses require a measure of belief.

Indeed, the experientially familiar distinction between the natural colors red and blue is scarcely apparent when we compare their quantifiable properties. Indeed, we find that the material formulation only remotely resembles the usual experience that we already have of the color. Therefore, we must directly and impartially engage the phenomenon itself If we wish to discover what it is really like because we cannot translate a numerically based analysis back to a visual experience of comparable merit. This is because intrinsic distinctions are not physical, and their nature is too subtle to be fully represented within solely material coordinates.

Thus, we recognize that an analytical representation of a color is merely a matter of convenience: a shorthand reference. Indeed, comparison between the actual, direct experience of phenomena and numerical value clearly reveals that the physical aspects of something that is essentially materially elusive, is not truly representative of the whole. In other words, the materialistic assumption that significance is solely physically represented is erroneous, and the partial reduction of phenomena into incompletely representative properties is an insufficient metric because it fails to express sufficiently the otherwise directly known condition. That is, the color formula does not reveal that which we know of the profoundly intrinsic nature of color from our own direct experience of its qualitatively descriptive condition. Clearly, therefore, significance is not entirely physical, and the material portion of things inadequately represents the profundity. Indeed, the physical is only remotely commensurate with the subtle, essential qualities of things.

Yet, the exclusively physical approach continues to be used to interpret existence conceptually on the basis of the quantifiable properties of things because they are most susceptible to analysis and classification. But the concrete does not exist independently of the entirety of the phenomenon. In fact, the qualitative nature of something pre-qualifies its existence in terms of significance. It is for this reason that the modern materialistic perspective, extrapolated to explain existence, causes life to appear meaningless. Existence is only partially and improperly represented if only explicitly tangible considerations are accommodated.

A portrayal of life established predominantly upon material conditions, in which the essential qualitative proportion is dismissed, describes merely the bare bones. Indeed, if we consider any object and intentionally overlook the character, timbre, and intrinsic nature that promotes its expression, we impoverish it to such an extent that it becomes a meaningless thing. However, if we wish to represent the intrinsic nature of something accurately, or even a particular person, we must find an appropriate medium that characterizes the qualitative and essential distinction. But since the quality of something exists intangibly, and is only obliquely revealed through quantification, there is no justification in reducing everything into quantifiable terms. Indeed, upon that basis, some kind of hypothesis must be constructed to abridge the discrepancy between the material abstraction and reality because the material husk and the substantive crucial identity will be at odds.

In other words, quantification only acknowledges those aspects of something that are amenable to physical measure. If we assume that our calibration of a color is a viable substitute for the qualitative dimension of the color itself, we remain oblivious to the authentic nature of the phenomenon and our understanding of existence is correspondingly compromised.

The medium whereby we communicate the intrinsic distinction of something that is essentially intangible must be metaphorical and figurative because these are the artistic means whereby the physically elusive is portrayed. Mechanical and mathematical representation pales dismally in comparison because intangible, intrinsic significances cannot be physically determined, and consequently, they are neglected from the equation. Thus, when we exclusively pursue the material condition as if it were the entirety, we become preoccupied with a merely peripheral representation, while the reality remains beyond the scope of the narrow view.

In other words, when a color is imagined as being entirely represented through numerical substitution, it loses the qualitative and intrinsic significance that is its authentic identity. Conversely, when it is characterized metaphorically and figuratively, the resultant portrayal reveals the essential distinction that differentiates one color from another. Consequently, a successful description of the physically elusive, qualitative relevance of something becomes experientially more meaningful to us because it reveals the full dimensionality, as opposed to merely the bone-dry physical conditions.

Thus, when the intrinsic qualitative significance of a phenomenon is discovered through immediate engagement, we do not require a philosophy of interpretation to give it substance because we already discern the significant proportion that otherwise escapes the perfunctory view.

In other words, the significant dimension of something resides within the qualitative value and the elemental distinction, both of which are intangible. This is important to recognize because it is the substantive condition of the existence of a phenomenon that is meaningful and consequently speaks to the similarly profound within the human constitution.

The substantive value and distinction of something is the intangible epitome of its existence that must be directly experienced in order to be known. Thus, we recognize that the material aspects of a person or a phenomenon are merely the superficial proportion. Through human relationship, intrinsic identity is easily recognizable, or disregarded at our peril, but the intangible descriptive is less obvious in terms of other natural circumstances. Nevertheless, the essence of something exists intangibly as a particular significance and resides within an immanent, meaningful volume that becomes readily discernible through immediate cognition.

2. The Necessity of Soul Transformation

The value of immediate cognition rests upon the knowledge that it offers respecting the existence of an intangible, but essential volume of significance that supersedes a merely physical representation. That dimension occupies a condition of immediacy wherein the intrinsic distinction of things is qualitatively represented.

It is easy and extremely simplistic of the materialist to insist that nothing exists beyond that which is physically verifiable when in reality we directly engage intangible significances almost constantly in everyday life. Superficial physicism reveals the alarming degree of abstraction that has overtaken the modern mind when we contradict our own directly ascertained knowledge with a contrived philosophical simplification. However, the shallow view and subsequent materialistic extrapolation also weighs heavily and unhappily upon the human heart because existence, viewed superficially, renders life seemingly meaningless.

It is disturbing to consider and observe the consequences of a perspective towards existence that is primarily preoccupied with the physical appearances of things. For example, an essentially futile transient perspective of existence tends to negate the importance of ethics and the aspiration towards a more noble culture, and we confuse freedom with self-indulgence.

Indeed, when we contemplate the deplorable human conduct in the world that nevertheless masquerades as tolerable, it is hardly surprising if we conclude that our impending prospects are negligible.

Obviously, humankind must advance qualitatively because our nature is insufficiently prepared for a substantive future. But the constraints imposed by materialism, through existential ignorance, upon qualitative, human development are further exacerbated by a regressive emotional condition of self-first that promotes an untenable self-absorbed mindset.

One helpful way forward towards a substantial and viable human future lies with the development of the capacity of immediate cognition. Thereby, we discover the authentic constitution and intrinsic volume that underlies the blatant appearance of things. Thus, the merely temporal and superficial perspective is subsequently revealed as wholly inadequate, and we recognize the vital importance of establishing a perspective towards existence that is both penetrating and intrinsically meaningful. Indeed, we need to know the actual condition of things because our present trajectory founded upon existential ignorance bodes very badly for the future condition of humanity. It leads towards a state of severe regression and subsequent mental and emotional bondage to considerations that are without worthwhile merit.

However, while immediate, experiential cognition through the focus of the authentic distinction of the individual human being, enables us to engage and recognize the substance of things, an emotional immaturity continues to obstruct existential progress. Consequently, an underdeveloped mentality that thrives predominantly on temporal indulgence hinders advancement towards the establishment of respective liberty because we remain oblivious to the vital significance of qualitative improvement and of our singular and collective potential.

At present, the predominant disposition of the human soul is frequently characterized by a self-centeredness that is remote and estranged from awareness of the full dimensionality of existence. It assumes that selfishness is inevitable because it imagines that if the shallow appearance of things is the full measure of their existence, selfism is justified. Furthermore, self-indulgence is fancied to offer a respite and assuage a haunting inner poverty that arises from a materialistic view. But the superficial cannot essentially nourish except in temporary measure: a practice that requires continuous repetition.

Consequently, at this crucial time in our development, the obsolete condition of the human soul requires comprehensive transformation and reorientation. This is accomplished when existential uncertainty and estrangement is replaced with profound assurance in much the same way as a greater vista of meaningfulness opens to the observer through immediate cognition. But the soul alone cannot reconstruct itself because it does not possess an inherent alternative paradigm that is suitable for the necessary leap and recasting of its nature. Required is an existential foundation of goodwill reestablished upon an exemplary ethos. And nothing less will suffice.

The human soul cannot self-ameliorate its own moribund condition because if such a thing were already conceivable, it would hardly require redress. Further, the necessary transformation is not behavioral but foundational because the perspective of the human soul needs to become enlarged and reestablished upon a basis of confidence in its own essential significance and the quintessential uniqueness of everyone else. This is a tall order for anyone, but a successive disposition of the appropriate calibre is established on our behalf. Through immediate experience within the individual heart, an exemplary nature supersedes the egotistical perspective.

Thus, through the simple deed of straightforward sincerity, the heart finds itself exposed to an archetypal ideal that it has not yet achieved but towards which it will systematically progress. Steadily, the soul becomes assured and confirmed through the immediate experience of a new paradigm. Thereby, the new is revealed intimately and immediately through the heart as the human soul opens to its influence, and we find that we are redirected in an entirely tangential, developmental direction.

Whenever a discord is revealed to us through the disquiet of the human conscience, it may be transformed if we are willing to permit the immanent, exemplary disposition to inspire and establish a nobler perspective within our soul. Thus, the openhearted approach towards the immediate presence removes us from the murk of our own anxious self-centeredness through the influence of intimate reassurance that is synonymous with the supernal nature.

Furthermore, there is no necessity to denominate the supernal nature that we discover through openhearted sincerity because, inevitably, every portrayal is better revealed first-hand by individually determined knowledge. Indeed, through the confusion of materialism and entrenched dogma, personal experience is the better approach to understanding. In other words, the exemplary nature must become known to the heart in order to inaugurate the transformation of the disposition of the soul. If we attempt to limit deity through material precision or traditional doctrine, we move our attention away from immediate experience where the recasting of the soul takes place.

Historically, human redemption is a much confused subject, further misconstrued in modern times by liturgics and dismissively disparaged by an atheism that derides the seeming credulity of the religious devotee. This cavalier approach arises with some justification from a predictable distaste at the assumption of a supernatural universal panacea for human absurdity. But openhearted sincerity is not a supernatural incident: it is an event of internal coincidence between the essential human being and the epitome of its own eventual fulfillment.

If we recognize the impasse facing humanity and consider the options available, we soon recognize that the deficiency lies within the human heart itself and our subsequently impoverished mentality. The remedy is no simple matter. Indeed, it is grossly unreasonable to assume that a moribund mentality can accomplish a successive ethical disposition upon the strength of its own inadequate merit. Nevertheless, this remains a common misrepresentation. But in reality, the wisdom and goodwill required does not reside within the conventional human psyche. However, the exemplary nature that is essential in order to reorient the soul can be directly engaged and fully experienced by anyone at any time through openhearted sincerity.

It is difficult for us to grasp that our conventional oblique perspective towards existence is both too narrow and incomplete. Yet, by comparison, through immediate cognition, we discover that we really know very little concerning the inherent nature of phenomena because we are abstractly preoccupied with the physical properties and conditions of things.

However, we discover through direct experience that physical appearances belie a considerably more significant intrinsic dimension that qualitatively augments the material and constitutes the substantial nature of things. Further, if the appearance of something is imagined as representing the entirety, then the conclusions of an exclusively, physically based consideration will inevitably remain entirely physically comprised and antagonistic to other more subtle considerations.

Thus, we see that the material view reveals only part of the story. And in the light of immediate cognition, exclusive physicalism is revealed to be too shallow, even if properties are microscopically analyzed. In other words, the full dimensionality of something is not represented sufficiently on the face of things but is only revealed to the observer through an entirely more penetrating way of looking.

The approach of immediate cognition requires the untrammeled engagement of the observer, whereby things are viewed uniquely as if for the first time without the hindrance of preconceived supposition. Physical circumstances serve as an anchor of our attention, but we seek to discover the intrinsic nature of the phenomenon that is not obviously represented by the appearance.

Similarly, the intrinsic significance of a person is of vastly greater significance than the physical representation. Indeed, we know well through human relationships that the appearance is but the tip of the iceberg and it takes time to know someone properly in order to establish a meaningful friendship.

However, empirical research in itself does not presuppose that the observer is now fully accomplished, or that observational sophistication is the same as developmental maturity. But is does furnish us with a measure of certainty concerning the otherwise overlooked immanent profundity of existence and to recognize an extensive meaningfulness beyond the obvious appearance of things. These insights establish a foundational premise of confidence in the certain existence of an immanent volume wherein the meaningful proportion of all things reside.

Therefore, recognizing that the qualitative development of the soul is the urgent priority of our time, we soon discover an inner way forward from the present impasse that bedevils healthy human progress. Nevertheless, we cannot reestablish our own soul according to the metrics of a maturity that we do not possess. The moribund mentality that confines and subjugates humanity does not contain the crucial paradigm required in order to transform successfully our present perspective of egocentricity, towards altruism. However, through sincere, openhearted sincerity, we discover an ethos of amity and selflessness as an immediate presence accessible through receptivity within the human heart itself. And therein resides the archetype of our own potential character without which humanity cannot meaningfully progress.

Thus, through sincere engagement, we advance in terms of an authentic integrity and by means of our steadily improved disposition, a meaningful condition of existence becomes increasingly acute and accessible to us. Therefore, whenever a regressive condition of soul arises, we turn within with a receptive heart and through our own choice, our condition of soul is transformed and we become appropriately reoriented through the immediate experience of the supernal nature.

The necessary restructuring of the soul involves a concise event of a choice between our characteristic, defensive behavior and the possibility of an exceptional mien of which we were formerly unfamiliar. Our task is to consent to the adoption of the condition of soul that is epitomized by the immanent, exemplary presence because, of ourselves, we are incapable of establishing a progressive demeanor that we do not intrinsically possess. Consequently, while human will alone is powerless to recondition the soul, nevertheless, we can choose to allow the necessary adjustments to our character and mentality. Thus, while we cannot foresee the necessary future condition of the soul from the view of our former constitution, we assent to its investiture through experiential pre-perception. This is the dynamic whereby our soul is appropriately reestablished towards a meaningful future and the further human development of cognitive and existential autonomy.

Interestingly, the instant of choice remains significant, even if the event of a misdeed or of acrimony occurred in the past and endured merely as a disturbance of guilt or resentment. That is, through the disquiet of the human conscience, an incident continues to prevail into the present. But through openhearted sincerity, it will be seen differently. Indeed, addressed in the manner of any inconsistency between the human soul and the supernal nature, through consent we permit the inspired successive perspective to supersede grievance and hatred. As a matter of fact, it is astonishing the good that occurs, even in our everyday lives, when we permit the supernal nature to reconstruct our hearts.

This will be a disappointment to those who had imagined that they could progress towards cognitional and existential autonomy solely through their own merit. However, if we glance at the world around us, we see the lamentable results of those efforts of self-amelioration and the delusions and distortions that accompany humanly contrived structures that promise easy improvement. Furthermore, if we endeavor to establish a progressive point of view founded upon our own beliefs and convictions whether they be atheistic or religious, the imaginative nature and origin of our abstract arrangement will ensure the establishment of the same disposition as that from which it is derived. Thus, self-righteousness, puritanism and a sanctimonious self-satisfaction will constitute the perspective of the religious zealot while complacency, intellectual conceit and materialism denote the staunch atheist. It all depends if our objective is a short-term bandaid or a truly profound reorientation towards a meaningful future that thankfully rests in better hands than our own.

Unfortunately, there is no longer sufficient leisure or latitude to debate the existence of a deity, nor any significant purpose if our convictions are stubbornly founded upon lame, materialistic prejudice and if our minds remain impenetrable to reason. It has been extensively emphasized here that the recognition of intangible significances is solely achievable through direct experiential cognition and, consequently, insight requires immediate engagement. It is the same with respect to openhearted sincerity in the sense that ultimately it is something that must be tried in order to be proven.

The necessary transformation of the human soul is not convincingly accomplished through any human agency because we do not possess the aptitude nor the endowment to redress our own existential isolation. Nor do we own the prerequisite knowledge concerning our future state or the means to replace our existing, obsolete condition of soul with the optimum condition that is appropriate to the further qualitative development of the soul.

Yet, through our sincere and openhearted concurrence with the immanent principle, we advance in terms of constitutive incorruptibility. This is not sentimentality but the entirely deliberate determination to embrace a necessary substantive soul-reestablishment. Furthermore, by virtue of an improved disposition, knowledge of the authentic condition of ourselves, others and of phenomena becomes steadily more attainable and acute because our disposition is proportionally ethical and increasingly less sullied by the former obsolete mentality.

Thus, we discover that experiential knowledge of intrinsic existence through immediate cognition expedites and reinforces the transformation of our soul. Through insight, we engage the more profound proportion of existence, which is encouraging, but not indispensable. Of greater precedence is a transparent heart towards the supernal nature.

However, the immediate experience of the essential, meaningful condition of existence is exponentially expanded to the degree that our conjunction with the exemplary principle is experientially justified. This is because individual right-thinking and feeling inevitably coincide with openhearted sincerity. Thereby, the subsequent transformation of our moribund mentality is progressively ensured. Indeed, we require neither belief nor faith in the usual sense because we are able immediately to experience these things through open-hearted sincerity. Thereby, a locus of trust is established, and through immediate engagement, we are able for ourselves to decisively and conclusively authenticate the existence and nature of supernal integrity and goodwill.

3. The Human, Singular Significance

By immediate cognition, we are able recognize the existence of the profound yet intangible proportion of phenomena, and we can extend the practice to include a more complete view of ourselves and our fellow human beings. To discern, through insightful consideration, the immutable distinction that resides independently of the corporeal condition, and to realize that everyone of us is of equal significance is an act of will that already suggests a predilection for the meaningful over the superficial. Thus, we find that the cursory appearance of all things belies a substantial dimension that exists intangibly and qualifies the physical with dimension. In this sense, the essential distinction of things is the substance, while the appearance represents the external shell.

Contemporary man increasingly believes that existence is entirely physically composed and that the self is a consequence of biological and neurological coincidence. This view loosely describes the corporeal condition within predictable material parameters, but it overlooks the existence of the essential crux of the human being that is the host of the human constitution. Indeed, materialistic western philosophy has become so strongly entrenched that many find the concept of non-material existence an inconceivable and irrational excess. As a consequence, to the degree that we concur with the narrow view, we deny our own substantive being and we are misled to conclude that humanity is essentially negligible.

The common present-day inability to distinguish

and straightforwardly identify intangible existence demonstrates the inadequacy of conventional cognition and further reveals a tendency to confuse profundity with ephemeral imagination. Additionally, in part, the adoption of a contrived philosophy established upon logical but materialistic thinking and perception, exacerbates a lopsided view because it fails to differentiate between directly acquired knowledge and thinking that is remote from the actual event. Furthermore, the advocate of materialism ignores entirely the existence of himself, the thinker, and contradicts the implication of the existence of the one, who is, at this very moment, engaged in the process of deliberation. It is as if a driver were to reflect upon the structure of a moving vehicle but fail to include himself at the wheel.

Yet, if the philosopher were to restrain conceptual abstraction beyond his own orbit for a moment, and directly observe the incidence of his own consciousness, the strange construct of the human being without a host would be stood on its head. This fundamental error of perception arises because of a widespread propensity towards conjecture that is isolated from the actual circumstances. But it is not through the imagination nor by abstract deduction that we grasp the nature of actual existence, but through immediate, experiential engagement.

Predictably, the superficial thinker is selective in terms of the evidence that may be included because, as a materialist, physically elusive data fails to correlate with the exclusively tangible nature of the parts under consideration. Thus, if solely material conditions are considered consequential, then the resulting conclusions will reveal an inevitably physical bias. There will be no mention of qualitative value or of the inherent nature of things, much less the existence of human individual and particular distinction, essentially untrammeled by material coordinates.

Nevertheless, through immediate, experiential reflection, we discover our own unique singularity of existence and thereby recognize that ultimately, the human entity is not corporeally dependent but inhabits a condition wherein all things exist imminently.

Thus, the popular concepts of life and death, and reincarnation are rendered parenthetic by the evidence of the experientially qualified recognition of our own unique being-ness. We discover through immediate cognition that the human singular distinction of existence itself resides in perpetual, incorporeal circumstances even though, through our corporeal status, of necessity, we remain almost exclusively absorbed and preoccupied with the physical. Furthermore, search as we may, we recognize through direct self-engagement that the unique individuality is not found anywhere within the bodily constitution but is only supposed to exist there through the abstract view of the determined philosophical materialist.

In other words, intrinsically, the body does not possess a specific identity, but merely exists as a biological commonality. Indeed, even though we almost constantly identify with it, it cannot claim to be a self. Not so the atypical identity of every human being: each person is bestowed with extraordinary singularity, evidence of which is incontestably demonstrated every time we refer to ourselves as "I".

It is from the perspective of the essential, incorporeal significance of our identity that we are able to recognize the intrinsic manner of the existence of others and the elemental state of phenomena. Furthermore, immediate cognition allows us to differentiate between significances and to distinguish one entity from another by virtue of the profound nature of their being.

The exploration of the profound state of existence through the direct, experiential engagement of the singular significance of the individual is a practice of cognition that is, paradoxically, wholly objective. The authentic condition of existence of the human being is able to recognize experientially its own uniqueness without recourse to reasoning and, similarly, immediately discern the essential particularity of other entities and phenomena.

In other words, it is from the position of our individual distinction that we are able to experience directly the inherent substance of things. And it is through the immediacy of the approach that objectivity is possible, while oblique and subjective reason and feeling-evaluation are temporarily restrained in order to permit a purely straightforward encounter.

Reason is ultimately only *imagined* possessing cognitive impartiality. In reality, the only area where calculation can claim neutrality is that of mathematics because the computation of numeric value is definitive. Nevertheless, conceptual deduction is imprecise. Logic, therefore, is mistakenly elevated as the ultimate cognitive authority, while, in fact, rationale is enormously flexible and oblique.

That is to say, the human being can evaluate

circumstances indirectly through the corporeal faculty of reason, but deduction concerning things remains essentially incommensurate with directly ascertained knowledge because a faculty such as reason, unlike the human entity, cannot directly engage. Similarly, our feeling-sentient, evaluative ability is necessarily a subjective, cognitive practice because it appraises circumstances from the perspective of preference and prejudice.

The essential existence of the human being is neither function nor faculty but exists as an entity. Only the unique individual is able to directly engage and immediate experience phenomena and, consequently, the essential human being alone is capable of entirely impartial cognition. That is to say, an entity is able to straightforwardly encounter something without evaluation because it restrains conventional cognition in order that its approach may be pure and free of distortion. Thus, the essential human being recognizes things in their extant condition for their qualitative and essential significance of existence.

But the approach required in order that the quality of the soul may be transformed and re-establishment upon an appropriate ethos is openhearted sincerity. Thus, the soul and the human ipseity become increasingly consentient and thereby progress is assured towards the realization of an entirely unforeseen human destiny under the aegis of immanent goodwill and wisdom.

4. Openhearted Sincerity

As with all intangible phenomena, there appear to be two ways that the essential condition of something can be conclusively verified as extant. One is by their effect, and the other is through immediate cognition. Through openhearted sincerity towards the immanent presence, we qualify the direct experience of the supernal nature by the changes that we discover within our own mentality and the corresponding timbre of our everyday lives.

But the approach of immediate cognition poses different challenges. Prerequisite to the effective practice of direct discernment is the establishment of our own singular distinction of existence as our cardinal cognitive perspective. The essential view is possible when we inhibit all interpretative and associative perceptive approaches and engage circumstances without the intrusion of predetermination or affective evaluation. Thereby, we engage phenomena directly and immediately from the straightforward perspective of the intrinsic significance of our own being.

On the other hand, the process of qualitative soul transformation occurs significantly through the heart because it is there that the former and now moribund mentality was similarly first cultivated. That is to say, in order to inaugurate the development of a successive disposition through openhearted sincerity we must directly engage the immanent principle that, in point of fact, epitomizes our own potential future nature.

However, at first we may feel off balance and without explicit coordinates, we might distrust the efficacy of our practice. But, when in doubt, and confronted by detractors regarding our unfamiliar position concerning the nature of existence, we can retrace our steps and return to those original certainties that we already know prevail beyond doubt. Through immediate cognition, we recognize emphatically that the essential existence of things is utterly real, and conclusively justified on that basis, we can adjudge the authenticity of all other things. Thus, we may return to the practice of immediate cognition and rediscover the unique distinction of phenomena, that precedes the physical in proportion and significance. Thereupon, unshaken, we resume our researches with renewed determination.

In other words, immediate cognition implicitly reenforces substantive experiences that may be otherwise difficult to justify. Thus, while openhearted sincerity is of greater significance because it transforms the qualitative timbre of the human soul, immediate cognition is suitable for the modern mind that doesn't believe casually but must have proof. Thereupon, the former approach towards human betterment becomes considerably more acceptable.

Furthermore, the practice of openhearted sincerity towards the immanent presence is of itself reassuring. Indeed, when the heart is rendered vulnerable to supernal influence, the effect of the consequences of goodwill upon the human heart is astonishing. And this has significant repercussions within our everyday life in every area that we open to the intervention of immanent caritas.

However, in terms of immediate cognition, the discovery of the human, essential ipseity, without the establishment of a commensurate ethos, can generate egoism because the individual, unique distinction can seem to the petty self to be a solely exclusive condition. Thereupon, the petty self assumes a degree of eminence that it is neither earned nor appropriate. Indeed, the reality is that everyone is possessed of an essential and particular distinction, whether they are aware of it or not.

Nevertheless, it is crucial that the authentic identity of the human being becomes our cognitive viewpoint because otherwise the discovery of the definitive nature of the existence of things remains remote. Thereby, the reality of an intangible volume of meaningfulness that is qualitatively established, becomes harder to appreciate. Furthermore, the existence of an immanent principle accessible through openhearted sincerity must remain a matter of faith until it is tried respectively and found to be real.

Therefore, the reason why we curtail intellectual activity and constrain the human, feeling-sentient nature is because they otherwise detract from immediate cognition. They are obliquely functioning capabilities and approaches to understanding that operate circuitously. That is to say, thinking and feeling are indirect and do not engage circumstances directly. Consequently, they are only indirectly active: they evaluate and calculate, but otherwise they remain unable to emphatically and pragmatically engage the intrinsic significance of things.

Thus, the difference between conventional cognition and direct engagement lies in the immediacy of the approach. Immediacy occurs between the authentic, human entity itself and the phenomenon, and not merely indirectly through the corporeal faculties and functions of the intellect and feelings.

We discover the human singularity through immediate cognition, and the ipseity is found to possess absolute authenticity. Consequently, we determine the value and merit of everything else from that position of existential assurance. The one thing that we can rely upon is our own singular and unique existence, and that of other people, and upon that certainty, we are able qualitatively to evaluate other philosophical and religious positions and determine their credibility.

In other words, the immediately ascertained, unique human singularity, which is the ipseity, is fundamentally positioned as the basis of our cognitive perspective. Thereupon, we establish our authentic identity as our cognitive locus and the singular distinction of the human being becomes the benchmark of our attention from where all things are directly experienced and evaluated for their significance.

To reiterate, the establishment of the human, unique identity as the ultimate, cognitive perspective of the individual is ultimately inevitable because it is the authentic entity of each of us. However, the mere experience of our uniqueness is, of itself, only marginally significant because of the seductive appeal it holds to our petty nature, and only accentuates self-indulgence. Furthermore, if we remain preoccupied with the wonder of our own existence, we become absorbed in the manner of the Eastern mystics, unaware of the greater significance of the discovery. But if, after the identification of our singular distinction, we position our integral identity as the cognitive view-point of our person; we engage phenomena from a position of absolute certainty.

Heartened by these profound experiences of human immutability, we yet remain obstructed by the recalcitrant soul and, consequently, we are unable to maintain the necessary cognitive consistency essential to the achievement of autonomy. The human soul is the poignant dimension of our existence that, at this time, finds itself estranged and vulnerable to confusion through its present isolation and ignorance. It exists in a condition of apprehension because it is removed from the full dimensionality of human potential and usually only experiences its own very subjective perspective.

Thus, the famished soul seeks respite within narrowly demarcated, corporeal conditions of existence and secures none that effectively assuage its feeling of privation, but finds itself compelled to reenact the same unfulfilling experiences over and over. However, through the sincere and openhearted approach, the soul becomes reestablished upon the unequivocal goodwill of the immanent principle which becomes the successive counsel of the human psyche supervising its perfect development.

Thus, all things appear in an entirely different light when the heart of the soul is reoriented in accordance with the qualitative disposition of the exemplary supernal nature. We find that we are no longer protective and defensive because the petty sense of self that required vigilant reassurance is steadily superseded by a more mature complexion established upon unequivocal amity and goodwill that eventually unfolds as the human legacy.

Indeed, our interpersonal human relationships are conducted in an altogether different manner than formerly. For example, if we harbor a resentment towards someone, our conscience provokes our attention. We recognize through our disquiet that we are, in a sense, ensnared and preoccupied with anxiousness, and consequently, we feel downcast. In this respect, the conscience should be heeded as an invaluable imperative that brings matters of imbalance to our attention. It is true that awareness of the distinction between right and wrong can be disregarded and banished from our awareness, but the consequences of the neglect of the conscience are cumulative, eventually precipitating an unsound mind.

However, now we open our heart to the immanent principle and in our sincerity, we directly experience a poignant understanding of the conditions surrounding the wrongdoing, and we see the greater perspective. It is as if it no longer mattered that we were offended or maligned, but instead we recognize the authentic condition, both of the person and of their plight, and our own considerations. Thereby, the resentment diffuses, and the heart accordingly softens, making it even more receptive to supernal intervention. Indeed, a very real healing of the soul takes place. Thereby, we find that essentially we are no longer defensive because that which we feared is seen differently and in true perspective because in the supernal presence, we are secure. Thus, through the agency of openhearted sincerity, forgiveness is both complete and absolute, and our own condition of soul is thereby profoundly gladdened.

Thereafter, we carry our misdeeds not as a canker but as healthy remorse and well-received contrition that dimensionally enhances our quality of soul because it instills modesty and perspective. Thereby, our former reactive and defensive stance is replaced with compassion and forbearance. Furthermore, inevitably there occurs an extraordinary event of exoneration, whereupon conciliate kindness and goodwill is even reflected serendipitous in our everyday circumstances.

These examples demonstrate the dynamic whereby the human soul is transformed from a former limited and self-circumscribed mindset, to where we participate in a definitive perspective and a magnanimous ethos. Moreover, the relinquishment of apparent self-determination merely parallels the educative process of a child who must abandon infancy in order to become fully developed. Thus, we recognize the all-important task facing humanity, and upon reflection, we realize that there is no realistic option: humanity must mature profoundly in order to advance meaningfully. And the transformative process begins within the heart of the individual.

Our shortcomings are revealed through our conscience, and within a sincere and receptive heart, they are successfully ameliorated. We find this to be an indispensable undertaking towards existential and cognitive liberation because we are otherwise hindered from realizing our full potential and we remain infantile: unfortunately, a sadly all to common incidence. Consequently, grow-up we must, and as we embark purposefully upon this greatest of all adventures, we find that soul transformation is both progressive and self-perpetuating through the extraordinary changes that subsequently take place.

5. The Supernal Presence

The direct experiential discovery of the fact of one's own singular distinction of existence is of significant importance in terms of the practice of immediate cognition. Thereby, we discover the crucial condition of phenomena because predictably the human essential ipseity sees all things originally and elementally. Consequently, upon a foundation of profound insight, one accepts easily the premise that the human heart can serve as a direct conduit between the individual and the supernal nature because we know for ourselves the existence of such things. One does not rely upon blind hope or religious belief, but we approach the matter with easy confidence.

Nevertheless, all this depends upon one's objective. Some people are quite content with the status quo and the supposed development of character according to an ideal nature does not seem to justify sufficiently all the effort that is required. That is as it stands: one really never knows the real circumstances of someone else's inner life, and it is arrogant to assume that we might. However, we are dealing here with nothing less than a complete turnaround of the human constitution in order that we may develop beyond the restrictiveness of a moribund nature that goes against our highest interest. In other words, humanity is at an evolutionary impasse because we cannot meaningfully proceed while we remain obstructed by our own insufficient mentality.

In other words, there are myriad influences that wear and tear upon the soul, and few of them are sufficiently coordinated with the requisite of qualitative improvement. Consequently, what is required is an overall focus, whereupon every inclination is integrated towards the same objective of qualitative progress. Indeed, we cannot presume to know the nature of the improvements that may occur because, from our present point of view, it is not within our competence to anticipate the completion of psychical renewal. For this reason, it is wonderful indeed to discover the way of openhearted sincerity and thereupon relinquish the consequences to the wisdom of far better hands than our own.

Openhearted sincerity towards the immanent exemplar that epitomizes the human future disposition permits the soul to relinquish regressive idiosyncratic tendencies. These blemishes are the inevitably persistent residue of a moribund psyche that accumulated under subordinate circumstances when the heart endorsed their consummation. Thereby, myriad dysfunctional and inappropriate behaviors developed and became the characteristic short-sighted human mentality. Once counterproductive mindsets and attitudes are established within the human psyche, they become the entrenched nature of the entity and they are not easily dislodged.

Clearly, many proclivities that may have seemed workable even at a very early age do not necessarily serve a meaningful future. In some cases, tendencies emerge that are blatantly destructive. Consequently, the establishment of a successive disposition must occur within the profoundness of the heart where the untenable present nature was originally conceived. Therefore, the renunciation of the moribund mentality requires unmitigated resolution, and if vestiges of the obsolete temper become evident, our part in the transformational process is a heart and soul willingness to allow the new to supersede the old.

In other words, the primary task of the individual is to initiate a comprehensive and wholehearted willingness, but otherwise to surrender the means of transformative accomplishment to the wisdom of the immanent presence. In this way, we recognize that the reestablishment of the human soul according to the supernal nature is not a magical event, but one that requires from us an absolute, individual resolve. That is to say, we must prepare ourselves through openhearted sincerity, but the necessary changeover is completed by supernal agency.

Obviously, the human dysfunctional mentality must be addressed and transformed, but we do not inherently possess the ability to recondition our own soul. However, when turmoil and agitation occur, our conscience immediately reveals the unquiet to us and thereupon, we wholeheartedly turn within, and through unconditional willingness, we ensure that our distress becomes mitigated through supernal influence. Thereby, we find that the old unworkable propensities wither and a new nature becomes increasingly characteristic.

Amelioration of the soul is obviously unsuccessful if we are not entirely sincere and if an authentic intimacy between the human soul and the immanent, supernal nature is not wholeheartedly established. However, as an encouraging benchmark, successful qualitative development of character is something that becomes quickly self-evident, and as a conscious event, we are well aware of its occurrence.

Thus, upon the conscientious application of openhearted sincerity towards the immanent presence, we find an appropriate disposition is steadily instilled as our accustomed demeanor and the former moribund condition of soul that formerly made ourselves and others miserable is mitigated. Furthermore, our point of view becomes progressively expanded and increasingly, with greater readiness, we recognize other people and indeed phenomena with respectful goodwill. Steadily, the soul becomes less egotistically oriented and defensive, and increasingly disposed to magnanimity and goodwill. Fittingly reestablish, it becomes calm because, through the assurance of the immanent presence at its very core, we are no longer apprehensive: we do not feel that we are alone.

However, in the same manner whereby we immediately engage a phenomenon objectively and empirically, and restrain pre-conceptual bias and preferential penchant in order to discover the authentic nature of something; neither do we wish to graft our own interpretation upon the supernal nature. We gain nothing through immediate cognition if we imagine that we already know what something is and, similarly, we cannot peremptorily gainsay the nature and influence of the immanent presence. If we knew already, we would be able to adopt a better disposition for ourselves of our own volition, and we would not need the guidance of a supernal paradigm.

The materialist imagines that the supposed, intimate experience of the supernal nature within the individual human heart is merely an overwhelming delusion perhaps akin to auto-hypnosis. This is because preoccupation with the obvious properties and attributes of things precludes the discovery of essential conditions. Consequently, the misgivings of the materialist are justified only from a superficial perspective. But, as we have already explored, materialistic Western philosophy is itself only tenuously supportable because it draws exclusively upon the most obvious physical condition of things.

      The materialist scorns the concept of incorporeal meaningfulness, imagining it to be an idea established merely upon wishful thinking and make-believe. But upon that basis, the intangible significances that one constantly encounters in everyday life must be similarly disregarded. Thus, materialism is recognized as a merely abstract construct that is preemptively antagonistic to empirical scrutiny and commonsense. Consequently, the narrow perspective should not concern us one iota, particularly as the transformation of the quality of the human soul is an entirely personal affair impervious to the comings and goings of fashionable philosophy.

6. Immediate Cognitive Engagement

The human ipseity always directly encounters the essential condition of phenomena because, in the manner of the quintessence of all things, it exists elementally. That is to say, the intrinsic state of all things is not superficial and merely physically apparent but possesses substantial inherence that, while implied physically, is only discovered through an insightful viewpoint. Thus, the human ipseity is the individual, emphatic declaration of individual existence that does not identify with the physical facade, but exists essentially.

In terms of immediate cognition, the intellect and feeling evaluation are restrained in order that the human observer may engage phenomena unalloyed by oblique reasoning, instincts and subjective preference. Thus, it finds things in their substantive condition as a similarly fundamental statement of existence alike, in that sense, to itself.

If we explore Nature from an original point of view and allow phenomena to speak for themselves, we discover an entirely different situation than that proposed by conventional scholarship. Our direct encounter reveals the circumstances of organic life without the elaboration of intellectual conjecture predominantly founded upon physical evidence. Therefore, by means of the immediate approach, we discern the full dimensionality of existence, including the intangible components.

Through the immediate cognitive engagement of a mineral, the observer discerns the inherent qualitative distinction that is the nature of the rock, as opposed to the material properties revealed through physical analysis. By the same means, direct observation of organic phenomena reveals the existence of a conceptual standard according to which an organism must comply in order to remain viable. That is, we discover an intangible imperative of arrangement and impetus that determines the manner whereby a living organism is conceptually anticipated and fully accomplished. If the constitution of the creature departs from the overall organizational structure, it inevitably fails and disintegrates. In other words, when an arrangement is no longer integrated according to the demands of organic organization, its existence as a living creature becomes untenable.

Thereby, we recognize the existence of an executive architecture, knowledge concerning which further reenforces the conviction of supernal continuity.

But we do not find the same regulation and superintendence in the mineral kingdom, nor does it apply to elemental existences such as the intrinsic identity of color or the intangible values of quality, intrinsic distinction and characteristic nature. They exist emphatically without an organizational institution. While they are similarly discovered and identified through immediate cognition, they are, nevertheless, recognized to possess original existence without conceptual composition.

Therefore, we distinguish decisively between elemental existence and conceptual architecture, or, in other words, as basic resources and structural expression, in much the same way as we recognize the difference between raw materials and man-made fabrication. In both cases, construction, whether organic or humanly fashioned, requires conceptual precedence. And no practical organization can occur without intentional conception.

It is through a comparison between the conceptual composition of organic phenomena and the innate, elemental existence of the inorganic, that we recognize the exhaustive and faultless intricacy of biological inception. As we increasingly grasp the significance of the existence of an impeccable integrity of origin that belies the blatant, material appearance and mechanics of an organism, through implication, we similarly discover intentionality.

In terms of the humanly manufactured item, we know that the existence of the finished object is founded upon conceptual inception. The completed article was obviously the objective of a preconceived idea and could not miraculously, somehow, fall into place through coincidental physical influences or capricious encounter. Such a proposition, although prevalent among abstract thinkers, is fiction, remote from what is actually taking place before us.

The Natural equivalence of the humanly conceived and manufactured commodity is similarly conceptual in origin. It is recognized through a qualitative comparison between the deliberately fashioned human product and the similarly explicit realization of organic organization. The two are found to be similarly deliberate, but the organism obviously remains independent of human invention and is recognized as alternatively conceived but conceived, nonetheless.

In terms of manufacture, human ingenuity and invention are only physically fully apparent when an object is fabricated and revealed. Although we cannot discern the conceptualization itself, we recognize it through the implication of the appearance of the finished product. Organic organization is similarly intangible, but it remains, nonetheless, entirely authentic. In both cases, through immediate cognition and the restraint of presupposition, the observer recognizes the existence of thought.

Through Nature, one discovers a perceptual gateway to intangible existences. This is of enormous significance because knowledge of the existence of a supernal mind no longer requires belief or faith, but the activity of genius is determined through immediate, experiential cognition. That is, the authenticity of intangible conceptualization is verified as extant through our own innate capacity of direct apperception. We discern the conceptual origin of the humanly manufactured article and, applying the same deliberation, we discover effective inception as the origin of Natural organization.

7. Materialistic Western Philosophy

A philosophical position that seeks to comprehensively explain existence in terms of exclusively material evidence is a willfully deliberate deception. Existence is not solely physical, and we know this from our everyday experience. In fact, everybody is aware of intangible nuances that lend dimensions of meaning to an otherwise bland carapace. It is as if material conditions represented the nouns, while the intangible proportions are the adjectives, metaphors and qualifiers without which the nouns would remain frozen.

In all likelihood, the motive for the materialistic slight-of-hand derives from a legitimate distaste for flimsy religious and superstitious testimony, and views of a similar ilk, including modern paganism. But the tragic consequence of the acceptance of a materialistic philosophy that purports to encompass all of existence, is to render life meaningless.

Certainly, we have no wish to contrive meaning where there is none, but materialistic Western philosophy, if it were an honest submission towards greater existential understanding, must append the caveat that it is a worldview established solely upon consideration of one category of data: namely physical existence. And if truthfulness were to become the new standard, the philosopher might add the qualification that the material is the tangible aspect of existence, but there exists a wealth of intangible merit that is incommensurate with the metrics of physical analysis.

However, a number of questions arise concerning the assertion of the existence of another significant proportion beyond the physical. But even the most abstractly preoccupied among us must concede to the existence of qualitative value. And indeed, the qualitative value of every phenomenon may be quantified to a certain oblique degree, but the reverse is not the case. That is, if we examine the numeric value of a quality, we do not discover the elusive nature of the phenomenon itself, but merely an incommensurate measurement of those gross properties that are susceptible to calibration. In order to describe the characteristic timbre of something, we must apply an appropriately corresponding narrative. That is, in terms of substantive value, we must utilize an illustrative description.

But there is always more. If we ask ourselves the question where does the elusive proportion that qualifies physical conditions with profundity and substance reside? We recognize immediately that, of itself, the qualitative value of something exists incongruously with physical proportions. That is to say, the essential nature of phenomena exists neither spatially nor within the constraints of duration, but immanently.

Now, if we reflect concerning the substantive merit of the individual human being, considering the manner of other phenomenal essential meaningfulness, we must conclude the same metric also applies with people. That is to say, the individual human being, by its unique respective distinction, possesses particular significance beyond the obvious appearance, and cannot adequately be described by quantification. And the answer to the question, where does the essential person reside, remains the same as before: within an immanent condition of existence.

The reason why this is important, is because an analysis of existence in terms of physical conditions and properties, philosophically extrapolated to encompass the entirety of existence as if that were indeed, the totality, is wrong. Thereby, we adopt a shallow view of the world wherein relevance is entirely lacking. Nevertheless, the materialist, using further legerdemain, claims the contrary: there is no need to despair, and then proceeds to list qualitative values that have been excluded from their own prior synopsis. Thereby, unawares, the exclusive perspective of materialistic Western philosophy is disproven. So what was the point of it anyway? And why is the concept of exclusive materialism defended with such determined vehemence?

It is difficult to offer specific answers to these questions, but a narrow abstract view often begets a similarly constricted and even defensive mindset. Perhaps the greatest concern has to do with the consequences that the pursuit of intangible values would imply. At present, substantive value can be acknowledged, but not allotted equal significance to the physical appearance of things. If the intrinsic nature of phenomena is accepted as an imperative descriptive of their intrinsic nature, then we must learn to navigate in entirely uncharted waters: a realm such as fine artists have to contend with.

But, we do not deny the existence of the physical. Indeed, the material serves as an essential navigational marker without which we would indeed flounder between nuances that we hardly can recognize or articulate. However, materialism and concomitant ignorance concerning the profound proportion of existence wherein value and meaningfulness resides, intensely alters the way in which we relate both towards life and one another. For example, if the intangible but essential merit of things is overlooked, then all forms of base crime become acceptable.

Indeed, it is indeed extraordinary and indicative of the pernicious nature of materialistic, Western philosophy, that we have managed to convince ourselves, against our direct experience to the contrary, that there exists no distinction between the human, intrinsic identity and the physical body. Materialism would have us see the organic structure without very many further consequences. That is, the biological vehicle is imagined to be without a host.

This position of self-deception merely demonstrates the inadequacy of materialistically prejudiced deduction. Abstract thinking, removed from context, argues within the limited parameters of chosen evidence, but then expands to encompass all of existence as if it were the definitive means of determining the extant condition of ourselves and of other phenomena. Thus, having resolved through a narrow view that intangible significances are without existential pertinence, we imagine the brain and its functions to be the seat of the human identity.

Be that as it may, the corporeal intellectual functions are unable to directly engage phenomena and they are incapable of immediate, experiential cognition. They must always work obliquely. Only the human entity itself is capable of direct cognitive engagement.

Therefore, in order to arrive at a logically conclusive evaluation, the materialist must subsequently disregard all evidence that cannot be definitively justified on those terms. Consequently, through materialistic prejudice, the means whereby we demonstrate the existence of something will be, inevitably, exclusively, physically dependent. For this reason, the abstract thinker logically concludes that intangible value is without pertinent significance. However, the exclusively physical results of the impartial investigation demonstrate a conspicuous superficiality and prejudice of perspective.

We are able to experience the intangible condition of things, but we are unable to verify their physically elusive existence from an exclusively physical perspective. Consequently, discernment of quality, value and the essential significance of the existence of things is inconclusive because we usually evaluate intangible merit, subjectively. As we know, subjectively derived evidence is disregarded by sophisticated opinion and although a complete denial is tempered by some commonsense, physically elusive evidence is nevertheless deemed unreliable. Thereupon, the significance of intangibly founded testimony is summarily dismissed.

While the subjective evaluation of the intangible dimension of phenomena does not seem to reliably compare with the decisively demonstrated physical condition, that does not necessitate its disqualification altogether, as if it did not exist. But that is precisely what materialistic, Western philosophy maintains. Materialism is a doctrine that is entirely established upon tangible evidence and therein lies its irrationality. Subsequently, an abstractly contrived, intellectual synopsis is established that is void of the full dimensionality of existence, remote from reality and, consequently, meaningless to the essential human being. Therefore, the intrinsic significance of existence is maligned merely because intangible value cannot be physically verified.

Convinced of the exclusive pertinence of the physical, we inevitably conclude that human identity is similarly limited to the obvious appearance. We select the brain as the most appropriate organ and imagine that our intrinsic identity is synonymous with our capacity to calculate and with the activities of our nervous system. Thereby, we avoid the discovery of our essential significance as a unique entity because our intrinsic identity does not exist physically. Yet, it is under the aegis of the human, singular distinction of existence that the innate significance of all other people and the elemental condition of phenomena is discovered.

The brain develops and coheres in unison with the corporeal entirety. It is tempered through the influences of congenital and developmental inheritance and by its own biography, alike to the rest of the organism. But the brain does not possess inherent distinction because it is an organ, not an entity.

The human brain is without a singular identity. But it is the essential individual alone who is capable of direct experiential engagement. The brain cannot engage circumstances but must obliquely sift and sort data. But it is only through the experiential encounter of an entity that things can be directly ascertained on the basis of their intrinsic significance.

Alone, through immediate, experiential engagement, the human, singular distinction discovers its own significance. It is from the perspective of our intrinsic identity that we are able to engage phenomena without the intermediary intrusion of the intellect or of sentimental evaluation. Thus, our encounter is entirely objective because it involves straightforward cognition between the intrinsic identity of the human being and the elemental significance of things. They both exist simultaneously in the same essential condition and, consequently, the cognitive event occurs without the need for analytical justification.

All physical appearances possess intangible value and unique significance. As a result, it is the intangible, qualitative dimension and intrinsic condition of the existence of things that holds the authentic distinction. In other words, the physically elusive value of something exists in the same element as the human entity. Consequently, the human being is inherently able to immediately engage a phenomenon and discover the full significance of its existence.

Through immediate cognition, we discover the qualitative distinction that epitomizes the nature of the existence of something. Thus, an encounter and subsequent recognition of the inherent condition of a phenomenon under the aegis of the essential human entity is neither detached in the conventional sense, nor partial, but it is an original event of cognition. Thus, the use of the terms *objective* and *subjective* is inappropriate because the actual distinction of something is discovered through an immediacy of engagement between essential existences. Thus, things are recognized for their inherent condition and, therefore, they are directly encountered as they exist inherently.

The excessive preoccupation with the physical

appearance of something is, itself, a prejudicial position. For example, if the gardener examines several hot peppers and wishes to distinguish between them, the objective approach requires some manner of independent calibration. If the distinction is to be founded upon the fieriness of the salsa, a profusion of a certain biochemical suggests that one pepper is stronger than the other. Conversely, the subjective procedure requires the gathering of alternative, human assessments that, through consensus, conclude which seasoning is fierce or mild.

However, neither approach identifies the inherent distinction between one pepper and another. The former avoids the intangible, qualitative significance altogether, while the other can never conclusively confirm the dissemblance. Meanwhile, the inherent particularity that distinguishes one pepper from another remains elusive because it exists elusively as a qualitative variance. In other words, intangible distinctions must be directly experienced in order to be recognized, but they cannot be definitively identified unless the human entity itself immediately encounters them. Thus, the human essential resides in a condition of immediate existence and engages and discerns the similarly essential condition of everything else.

Through an obsessive, material exclusivity, the human essential is denied its full significance. However, if the human being is comprised merely of corporeal characteristics, then our cognition would remain similarly constrained within the limits of our physical disposition. Immediate engagement would be correctly evaluated as merely subjectivity, although under a different name.

But the human being is incorrectly and inadequately defined upon the basis of physical appearance. Each human body has more in common than disparate from every other figure. Essentially, every corporeal constitution remains the same and that which does distinguish one person from another, is hardly sufficient grounds to justify the singular distinction that we recognize as our own uniqueness. In other words, there are innumerable bodies, but every human being rightly claims a singular identity. If this were not so, we would operate as a throng and not as individuals. We would function collectively, like an animal that possess only a common identity.

The application of immediate cognition requires the existence of an essential singularity that is far more profound than group identification or bodily appearance. It must exist autonomously and essentially in order that cognition be both individually distinct and elementally discerning.

The unique singularity of a person resides in a condition that is independent of his corporeal status. It is discovered emphatically through experiential directness and subsequently positioned as the sovereign, cognitive perspective of the human constitution.

Thus, through immediate cognition, the human essential person engages the central distinction of itself and other human beings, and the intrinsic significance of phenomena. Nevertheless, self-realization of itself is insufficient. If the human being remains selfishly preoccupied, then, inevitably, perception will be swayed by the egocentricity of a lesser mentality.

Fortunately, the optimum approach is the most

straightforward. Through openhearted sincerity, the soul discovers the immanent principle and, steadily, the egocentric mentality is superseded and personal integrity is simultaneously advanced. Thereby, the authentic identity of the human being becomes increasingly predominant while the counterfeit sense of self is abandoned.

Thus, we recognize two approaches towards the recognition of the intrinsic nature of existence. The one is dogged and purposeful but fraught with the possibility of self-deception because it does not consistently dissuade or supersede egocentricity. But the other addresses and amends the root imbalance of the human soul.

Thus, under the aegis of the supernal ethos, the human soul is entirely reestablished upon existential assurance, while egotistical misidentification is superseded by benevolence and unselfishness. Subsequently, the essential human being is established as the human, sovereign identity.

8. Materialism and Substance

The application and understanding of the term faith, in modern times, has come to imply an unequivocal certitude concerning the existence of something that cannot otherwise be substantially authenticated. From the perspective of materialistic, Western philosophy, blind trust is a commonplace designation that encompasses a diversity of irrationality extending from superstition to delusion.

However, the materialistic worldview rests solely upon physically corroborated evidence in order to prove the existence of something. But proving the validity of one thing does not necessarily disprove the existence of another. This is particularly the case in terms of those things that must be directly experienced in order to be known, and which require incommensurate metrics from the physical in order to be confirmed. For example, the omission of the qualitative significance of phenomena, the physically elusive value of circumstances and insight concerning the intrinsic distinction that differentiates one thing inherently from another, lies obliviously beyond the reach of physical analysis. Therefore, the establishment of material parameters confines research within a narrow radius, excluding the existence of those things that we know from experience to be authentic, and which suggest that existence is not merely physical. Further, it denies the empirically acknowledged dimension of existence that otherwise gives life its entire significance and meaning.

Materialistic, Western philosophy is able to promote a fundamentally contrived perspective towards life only because it indulges in a convincing, but abstract, polemic at the expense of empiricism. Only an abstractly conceived position could exclude the significance of the intangible and experientially recognized dimension of existence because it requires a particular, intellectual detachment that is estranged from common experience.

Thus, we find that the presumptuous trust of blind faith and the theoretical assumptions of the materialist, although the approach is different, actually have much in common.

In the abstract, the materialist further concludes that reasonable evidence does not exist to support an intangible dimension of physical existence. However, this indiscriminate generalization is obviously unsustainable because it is nonscientific and contradicts the discipline of empiricism. But the materialist counters that the experience of elusive value is necessarily subjective and, consequently, it is inadmissible as substantial evidence and, subsequently, dismissed as hearsay. But upon closer examination of the practice of subjective cognition, we recognize that while idiosyncratic intelligence remains unmanageable in the precise terms of a physically demonstrable event, nevertheless the fact of the existence of qualitative significance is arbitrarily repudiated only at the expense of rationality.

The abstractly preoccupied, conceptually speculative researcher, regards the deduction of exclusively, materially substantial evidence as the superior, cognitive approach to understanding. As far as materialism is concerned, maybe that's the case. But upon the strength of that premise, the self-evident condition of things then becomes philosophically extrapolated as if matter were the exclusive condition of existence.

Furthermore, the empirical approach readily reveals the authenticity of the intangible significance of phenomena, even though the intrinsic value of something can be neither measured nor calibrated in the manner of a physical occurrence. Indeed, good sense can reinforce subjective assessment and temper idiosyncratic evidence through the wisdom of accumulated experience. Thus, by pragmatism, we avoid possible distortion by unrestrained human evaluation.

Abstract logic, on the other hand, seems to imitate mathematical precision and offer certainty, but in reality it is based on persuasive polemics rather than on accuracy. Indeed, the truthfulness of an argument can never be definitively demonstrated as an equation, but, conversely, it relies primarily on the persuasive thesis of the defender. Indeed, accuracy and precision are not the same as reality, and may have no bearing upon it. Thus, we find that between the abstract methodology of deduction, remote from immediate experience, and logical expostulation, whereby a position is supposedly qualified by argument, the results may remain inconclusive and remote from experientially recognized conditions. By its remote functioning and the skewed disregard of the intangible and empirical dimension of existence, materialistically established logic is a far from a decisive practice in determining truth.

The convinced materialist views as blind faith any physically incommensurate concept and consequently approaches it with horror as if it implied trust in make-believe. Irrespective of an entrenched partiality that disregards all intangible, empirically recognized evidence as unproductive, nevertheless, the materialist claims a monopoly of judgment based upon the assumption that the entirety of existence is properly understood solely upon the evidence of the physical appearance.

In the same way, the conceptually preoccupied and abstract thinker fails to uncover the full extent of existence because of a prior evaluation which presupposes the condition of things. Consequently, through an entrenched bias, the abstract, intellectual approach towards understanding life is ill-suited to determine whether faith in something intangible is justified or not because reason is necessarily partisan by virtue of the way that it functions. In other words, the intellect cannot objectively evaluate a condition that is incommensurable with calculative, cerebral processes. Therefore, intangible existence can be neither justified nor denied by reason.

The discipline of scientific empiricism is undermined when it is used to uphold the authenticity of a philosophical assumption. Indeed, the empirical pragmatist is unhappy with conceptual presumption either in terms of religious belief or intellectual disengagement, and necessarily has to meet circumstances directly and experientially. But, through a direct open-minded approach, things are discovered in their profound state and assessed by the intrinsic nature of their particular existence. In other words, direct cognition does not allow pre-conceptual or sentimental distortion, but wishes to discover the authentic manner of the existence of things, as they are, in their own right.

Therefore, the study of physical conditions and the workings of phenomena should not be overextended as an existential philosophy because physicalism will always exclude the corporeally elusive significances that qualify the appearances of things with intrinsic and individual meaning. Physics is specialized insofar as it concerns the obvious properties of phenomena, but through the exclusion of essential relevance, a materialistically established philosophy inevitably distorts our understanding of reality.

There is nothing mysterious or mystical about the immediate approach, other than its unconventional character. Immediate, cognitive engagement determines what a phenomenon is through a direct, unbiased encounter. Allegiance to a humanly fabricated ideology, whether it be intellectually conceived or the subject of revelation, is irrelevant because through direct, experiential cognition things are discovered not as we interpret them to be, but in their original condition.

Thus, we move forward with our research with consistency and pragmatism without the hindrance of personal predilections or inclinations. Our intention is to discover the native condition of phenomena through our own cognitive autonomy whereby we establish an essential perspective and not one based upon the preconceived bias of accumulated scholarship or conviction. We recognized that a pre-established position will only distort direct cognition and, consequently, it is necessary to engage phenomena originally because only an open-minded, direct approach enables us to discover the authentic and elemental condition of things.

Modern understanding and the application of empirical evidence suggests that experimentation is always used to support a hypothesis. But if analysis and testing only concern the physical, the conclusion is inevitable and strongly persuaded by an existing mindset. Similarly, it is established practice that a conditional position should be submitted to the consideration of other peer professionals. However, in practice, a provisional outcome is already firmly entrenched through consensus concerning similar already accepted scholarship. Consequently, a new perspective must correspond with old established ideas. Otherwise, it is thrown out.

The materialist, in particular, confidently maintains that a hypothesis, supported through the consensus of peer authority is readily open to challenge and amelioration. In reality, an established position is not easily or willingly dislodged. Indeed, a philosophical opinion inevitably rests only upon uncertain evidence because of the nature of philosophy, but the onus is on the challenger to present conclusive, contrary evidence, or the prevailing proclivity remains in place.

Pure empiricism is the natural consequence of the establishment of the openminded position as the seat of the human, cognitive perspective. It involves direct observation and immediate experience and does not seek to evaluate a hypothetical standpoint. But in addition, from the standpoint of human ipseity, all things are originally encountered in their elementary condition as if for the very first time, without preconditions.

The experiential discovery of the human ipseity is the basic and indispensable precursor to immediate cognition. It is through the same existing elementary condition of the human and singular distinction of existence that the pragmatic yet subjective appraisal of intangible meanings is replaced by definitive knowledge.

Once the individual quintessence is established as a human sovereign locus, we find that we can no longer identify ourselves with any aspect of the physical body. That is to say, we have discovered our authentic significance and we find that it exists independently of the physical appearance. Thereafter, phenomena are not evaluated exclusively on the basis of their obvious condition, but for their immaculate existence, unalloyed through the pre-conceptual and interpretative processes of the intellect.

Human ipseity empirically engages its own existence and finds that the singular human distinction resides in an elementary condition and that the essence of all phenomena exists in the same way. Experiential immediacy reveals that the intrinsic human identity has an absolute and distinct persona. However, the feeling nature does not inhabit a correspondingly pristine condition but remains the resultant amalgamation of a long and confused, human biography. It is for this reason that the human soul requires supernal intervention and guidance through openhearted receptivity.

The sincere human being is perfectly aware of the defects of the soul, and attentive to the necessity of a revolutionary re-establishment of both conduct and attitude. The quintessence of the human, feeling nature is the heart and, it is through the heart that we discern the possibility of a new soul structure appropriate for a meaningful future. We experience these things immediately and adjudge their caliber through comparison. Under the aegis of the human quintessence, we are already cognitively familiar with the intrinsic nature of existence and it is an easy step to render the heart susceptible to supernal goodwill and wisdom.

Attentive to the essential nature of things as they exist regardless of our intellectual or subjective assessment, we discover a standard or a reference that epitomizes the nature of reality. This we use as a comparison in order to evaluate our experience of the supernal nature through the human heart. We perceive by immediate engagement, the elementary condition of things which builds within us a certain familiarity with intrinsic existence. Upon this basis all things are judged for their authenticity because we have developed a sense for reality and now we can tonally distinguish between abstraction and authenticity.

9. The Tenor of Authenticity

When the ipseity, which is the uniquely individual, essential, human identity, engages phenomena immediately and as if for the very first time, one is struck with astonishment because everything is found to possess intrinsic significance. We recognize that in the past we did not realize the existential inherence of things because we assumed a pre-conceived familiarity that influenced our perceptions. Moreover, we usually compared things with accumulated memories of similar phenomena that brought us to assume a knowledge of things without engaging them originally or deeply. Thus, we were concerned about our own evaluation to the detriment of knowledge by direct cognition.

Immediate cognition reveals the inherent meaning of phenomena. This is important in terms of the transformation of the soul because thereby we realize that there exists an immediate proportion of intangible value that gives the material appearance of things dimension and meaning. Consequently, upon the strength of immediately ascertained knowledge, the concept of the existence of an exemplary ethos that resides essentially becomes credible.

By itself, it is not necessary to develop the practice of direct discernment in order to approach the supernal exemplar within the human heart. Indeed, when once we have intimately engaged the immanent principle, there is no further doubt in our minds to contend with.

Nevertheless, through the nature of subjectively ascertained information and the manner whereby we can be easily misled by the convictions of others, it helps if we already possess the ability to differentiate between that which is intrinsically authentic and mere conjecture.

Familiarity with the tenor of intrinsic existence is a direct consequence of immediate engagement. Therefore, our knowledge is not derived from imaginative abstract or extravagant formulation, but by experiential recognition of the inherent condition of things. In the past, the usual approach was oblique, and we seldom engaged something without relying on the inference and reference of established assumptions.

Through immediate engagement, we bypass the conventional, cognitively oblique approach and casual perception that is influenced by pre-conceptual means and enter into an imminent agreement with a phenomenon. Thereby we discover the extant circumstances of the existence of things because essential significance exists implicitly as it is and not as we suppose or imagine it to be. Consequently, we engage a thing directly without the intermediary of preconceptions, interpretation or biased inclinations. Thus, the phenomenon is first found in its entirety as an existential declaration before being analyzed and dismembered in order to discover the mechanics and chemistry.

It is the conventional, abstract manner of human perception that obscures direct experience and the subsequent acquisition of essential knowledge. Removed from the immediate engagement with an event, through the substitution of an appellation and myriad subsequent associations, we remain ignorant of the inherent identity of a phenomenon because we have not engaged it directly or profoundly. The characteristic associated accumulation of retrospection that we accumulate instead of the actual occurrence, preempts immediately ascertained knowledge. But the abstract way by which we obliquely consider a phenomenon is a poor substitute for the direct cognitive encounter.

When we approach something from a position of ignorance, restricting our conventional cognitive practices, the human ipseity is able to silently and immediately encounter a phenomenon. Direct experience from the point of view of human essence takes the place of intellectual, subjective and emotional evaluation and we thus discover the same, existing elementary state of things.

Conversely, through the indirect assessment of a phenomenon, inevitably we will be mistaken concerning the deeper significance and suppose that our characterization of something is the authentic condition of its existence. Inevitably, the superficial circumstantial view relies heavily on the apparent appearance. Thus, we presume to possess knowledge that is in fact cognitively beyond the reach of our cerebral faculties and subjective perception. But more significantly, we subsequently construct an interpretation of existence that is equally negligible. We imagine that we grasp the entirety when in reality we are most significantly preoccupied with our own cursory assessment.

We used to represent things according to our own predisposition, our inclinations or the strength of a pre-established intelligence. Our assessments may even have been further qualified through scholarship and conviction. But even when they were supported by peer consensus, they remained in the dark if they were established without immediate and relevant correspondence. That is, the intrinsic and intangible distinction of phenomena is only authentically discernible by the immediate commitment of the essential human ipseity.

Unfortunately, when we assume that our identity is merely a consequence of our physical condition, inevitably, we evaluate phenomena upon those terms and conclude that the entirety of existence is exclusively, materially consistent. However, if we practice direct, experiential cognition and inhibit intellectual and subjective feeling evaluation, the first thing that we discover is our own elemental condition of existence and the similarly intrinsic condition of phenomena.

Engaging phenomena directly through from the perspective of the human ipseity, we discover the actual condition of something because we encounter it straightforwardly from the position of our own essential condition of existence. Thereby, we discover what a thing really is and what it signifies because we meet it essentially in the absolute and unconditional manner in which we ourselves exist and not merely in terms of the physical appearance.

It is appealing to the abstractly preoccupied philosopher to adopt an interpretive stance towards life and to elaborate and, thereafter, further advance a particular position. But any assumption about the nature of life will merely be an ambiguous philosophical proposition. It cannot be demonstrated as definitive because of the remoteness of intellectual estimation from the actual event. Therefore, it is further rationalized, and the arguments are arranged in a succinct and sequential manner in order to sway and convince associate scholars who are proficient in that particular speciality.

But none can conclusively demonstrate the legitimacy of an abstract concept because an elusive theory may be challenged or accepted only by the keen sense of peers, but not definitively proven. If it were proven, it would no longer be hypothetical.

Those who engage existence immediately and experientially, establish for themselves, through straightforward cognitive encounter, a familiarity with actuality that could never be attained through intellectual finesse. Reality has to be experienced directly because it is a condition or state of existence. The sovereign uniqueness of the human being alone is capable of immediate experience and through the ipseity of our existence that we are able to engage phenomena essentially, and thereby we directly discover the manner of their existence.

In order to discover the authentic condition that essentially and intrinsically distinguishes the existence of things, phenomena must be engaged without pre-conceptual assumptions. Original knowledge demands that the essential human entity be established as our sovereign perspective. Therefore, the intellectual faculties are restricted so that they do not interfere with the immediate engagement.

The essential human being is not an instrument or a physical device, but an identity of unique significance. A physical function does not possess singular significance and, consequently, it remains incommensurate with being. Similarly, and contrary to contemporary scholarship, the brain is a faculty of the body while the human ipseity is the lasting identity.

Human ipseity is the individual distinction of existence and, as such, it exists in an immediate condition from whence it recognizes the essential meaning of all others and things. If we imagine the brain as the seat of our existence, then we are really identifying ourselves with a biological vehicle that continually changes, but through immediate cognition we are able to differentiate between the intermediary and the intrinsic host.

Unfamiliar with a cognitive approach that is able to encounter phenomena directly and essentially, and mistrustful of our subjective, feeling-sentient evaluation of things, we imagine that the greater the intellectual proficiency the more successfully the riddles of existence are resolved. Thus, we abandon our sovereign, cognitive prerogative to the authority of a didactic intelligentsia and to the technical specialist, in the same manner as we abandoned our autonomy in former times to the cleric and to doctrinal orthodoxy.

The intrinsic distinction of a phenomenon is not discovered by reason or by examining the purely physical appearance of something because it does not exist superficially, but essentially. That is to say, one cannot recognize inherent significance through deduction and reason, because it exists not conceptually but pragmatically. The actual person is not the corporeal appearance or one of its organic functions, but it is the physically elusive quintessence that exists essentially as the human, individual distinction of existence. It exists elementally and recognizes the same profound extent in terms of all other things.

Physical conditions provide cognitive focus. We engage the phenomenon, but we do not occupy ourselves merely with the material. Thus, through immediate engagement the essential person discovers the intrinsic significance of things. The physical overlies the essential, but the human ipseity recognizes the significant distinction of a phenomenon because both exist in an emphatic condition of being and not merely superficially as a physical appearance.

10. Conventional Cognition

Conventional cognition habitually rests on prior understanding. It is indirect because it does not engage a phenomenon straightforwardly, but relies on the interpretation of a situation based on similar, recognizable conditions. Through straightforward encounter, immediate cognition avoids the oblique approach. Thereby, the human singularity, unlike the intellect or feeling-sentience, is able to directly experience a phenomenon and discern its intrinsic condition of existence.

When we restrict the habitual approach that usually prevents straightforward engagement, then our view is no longer obstructed by the assumption that we already know something about the object. In other words, the engagement is original. Consequently, the observation occurs between the individual and the thing without intermediary interpretation. For this reason, a cognitive event such of this concerns solely the essential person and the object, as opposed to the viewer inhibited by a variety of suppositions, associations and anticipatory conjecture.

Immediate cognition rests upon a simple premise. Normally we observe an unusual phenomenon and compare the new with previously assimilated intelligence, and our understanding builds upon prior experience. But immediate cognition differs because it encounters something afresh, as if for the first time. Thus, the original state of a phenomenon becomes obvious because we do not associate the present event with the preceding experience.

This reason why this is significant is because the direct approach is sufficiently atypical to cause considerable astonishment. Indeed, it is astonishing what eludes our attention by the assumption of prior knowledge. Thereby, we discover by immediate engagement the fact of the existence of an object, an experience that is breathtaking.

However, if this were the extent of direct engagement, we would rightly conclude that the immediate approach was nothing more than astute observation. But there is another component that makes the immediate encounter extremely unusual and it is the recognition of this characteristic which causes the most difficulty.

The conventional practices of associative cognition, measured evaluation and feeling-sentience are restrained. Thereupon, that which occupies the vacuum as the direct observer is the essential human identity. Subsequently, through direct experience, the human being discovers experientially its own unique uniqueness. Thereby, human identity transfers from the erroneous assumption that the corporeal faculties are the seat of our intrinsic existence and becomes autonomously reestablished. Furthermore, we recognize through imminent engagement that the human, unique distinction exists independently of our corporeal condition and possesses intransigent and unique significance.

In other words, when we inhibit the usual intermediary interference, we discover the condition in which things actually exist, including ourselves. This is the elemental view.

Obviously, the recognition of an autonomous

human ipseity throws conventional understanding into a turmoil. This is compounded when we discover that the essential person is able to discern the similarly intrinsic nature of other people and all other phenomena. Subsequently, a completely neglected dimension of existence becomes apparent and we discover that it is not the material appearance of something that is significant, but the intrinsic distinction.

Predictable uncertainty always accompanies conventional cognition, even where there seems to be clear and persuasive evidence. This is because everything is streamlined and assessed by the oblique functioning of the intellect and feeling-sentience. Consequently, a person will present a certain position with persuasive confidence that is exclusively founded upon deductive reason, imaginative conjecture, or inference established upon subjective feeling evaluation. But ambiguity is inevitable because the familiar cognitive approach is always uncertain by virtue of the indirectness of the assessment.

Immediate cognition from an unvarnished perspective is entirely different because of the straightforward nature of the encounter. We do not have to evaluate anything because the human essence engages circumstances without supposed foreknowledge and thereby, through insight, discovers the essential condition. Insight is possible because the human ipseity exists in a condition of immediacy with the elemental significance of all phenomena because it is itself primary.

Normally, we approach a situation in order to understand it, but not to discover what it in fact is. And accumulating overwhelming evidence to support a chosen view is a familiar strategy to obtain approval. It is believed that the greater the weight of favorable testimony, the more credible the finding. Consequently, it is a momentous task to argue against scholarship because of the sheer volume of circumstantial evidence that is thrown into the discussion.

Thus, a strange thing occurs. The researcher supports a selected point of view concerning existence with the endorsement of extensive acumen and auxiliary evidence. But the observer who approaches phenomena through original, direct engagement, discovers the existential profundity of circumstances. The scientist may be correct, but the normal approach concerns what a phenomenon is about, and not what things are and what is really going on. This happens because the usual approach contaminates the evidence through alleged prescience.

Materialistic Western philosophy is established upon the conviction that the physical condition of things is the full extent of their existence. This appears to be a rational position except that the evidence is exclusively drawn from the obvious properties of things because the intellect manages tangibly verifiable intelligence very logically. Furthermore, and most significantly, the observer who is preoccupied with his own point of view will not be able to recognize the substantive dimension of circumstances. And if that preconception is established on determined materialism because of an aversion towards things metaphysical, the consequences will be the predictably shallow worldview that we see today.

Predictably, an orderly philosophical construct strongly appeals to the intellect and the scholarly few enjoy the prestige of revelation. They are reluctant to permit a challenge to the abstract, intellectual construct and resist ferociously. Unfortunately, some antagonists merely dispute the unusual but avoid revealing their own central postulate. This may be through uncertainty and lack of clarity or perhaps they recognize that an argument founded upon exclusively material evidence is precarious through an obvious bias. Offense and ridicule in these circumstances appear the more prudent strategy.

The analytical approach can never reconcile with knowledge derived through immediate cognition when it comes to existential considerations because the two are incommensurate. That is why materialistic Western philosophy as such, is misleading. It is unfortunate, however, that a doctrine such as this has become ubiquitous because the superficiality erodes human emotional health.

Thus, the reasoned approach appears to reign supreme because through physical analysis and logical deduction we are able to systematically discover the elements of natural law and reapply our findings to our advantage. It appears, thereby that we understand the condition of the existence of phenomena while in reality, we only perceive their physical state, composition and subsequent functions. Furthermore, the intangible dimension of existence that is recognized through direct engagement, is maligned and disregarded because it is thought rest merely upon subjectivity.

However, the human, singular distinction experiences phenomena without the assistance of both the intellect and feeling-sentience. For example, through immediate cognition, we approach an organic form and recognize that which is not readily conspicuous through a scrutiny of the obvious appearance. For example, apart from direct engagement itself, which is an extraordinary experience, we discover further the conceptual nature of organic arrangement. That is, we discern the ideational volition that compels the particular expression of the form.

Thus, a plant moves by a progression of opposite expression through a process of constant metamorphic reestablishment. Upon germination, the seed transforms into the elementary plant. The rudimentary leaves diverge into a stem, further surrounded by leaves of greater form complexity, eventually culminating with the flower and the apogee of the seed once more. At every stage and at any moment the plant is always complete otherwise it could not transform into a different appearance. Consequently, at any point within the metamorphic succession, one may enter into the activity of ontogenesis and follow a part of the cyclical, sequential development. The never-ending progression is only further compounded by the introduction of a dynamic whereby ecological adaption is introduced through local influence and cross-pollination whereby the particular characteristic expression of the plant ideal, adjusts qualitatively within a contextual milieu.

Through the foregoing example we recognize that the progression of metamorphic transformation is accomplished through purposefulness and intent, indeed, otherwise only chaos would be apparent. Thus, through immediate cognition we discern the existence of an intangible, conceptual formulation at work, and instead of a solitary phenomenal appearance like that of a mineral, we discover in nature the existence of a dynamic of form dissolution and refashioning towards specific and consistent purposes. Thus, the conceptual structure that is discerned by immediate cognition is an entire cyclical configuration that occurs constantly and ubiquitously.

Spontaneous methodology and complex organization are inconceivable in human affairs and neither does impromptu order occur in Nature. When the integrity towards the ideal is compromised in Nature, the life-form perishes. Chaos is only prevented through an inherent insistence of conformity towards a conceptual arrangement that exists intangibly but whose mandate is recognized phenomenally.

The existence of an idea, recognized by its physical consequence, is incomprehensible without purposeful inception. Thus, it is through the immediate, cognitive engagement of the conceptual consequence that we discover the inaugural provenance of idea and volition. Through direct encounter and impartiality we recognize these things and we are not disturbed merely because the perspective is unconventional.

Both materialism and spiritualism are superficial points of view. The materialist abstractly conceives of an existence wherein everything is physical while the spiritualist imagines a condition wherein matter is extant but elusive and rarefied. The spiritualist and the materialist evaluate existence indirectly and conceptually, and strangely in terms of spiritualism, solely in physical terms.

However, in order to grasp the concept of imminent, intrinsic existence, it is necessary to engage things directly because otherwise this discussion remains but another abstraction, as remote from essential existence as materialism and spiritualism. But by immediate engagement, we discover that essential significances are profoundly more relevant than the blatant, material appearance. And it is well worth our while to try this approach for ourselves.

It is the same with respect to interpersonal relationships. If we consider the significance of ourselves and others in terms of the body, our correspondence will remain superficial. However, when we recognize the intrinsic, individual significance of others, our corresponding engagements will become poignant and meaningful.

When we preoccupy ourselves intellectually with conceptualizations concerning existence, we establish a condition of detachment wherein all manner of fiction may potentially develop without demonstrable justification.

However, human cognition is not limited to deduction and feeling assessment because, in spite of what we believe, nevertheless, each person possesses intrinsic, autonomous distinction. That is because, although commonly unrealized, the human ipseity is the absolute, existential foundation of our individual existence.

Immediate, cognitive engagement by the unique, intrinsic distinction of the human entity provides an unambiguous experience of our essential condition as an irreducible statement of existence. From the view-point of our own elemental status, we apprehend other phenomena immediately and find similarly essential distinctiveness. Cognitive immediacy reveals the dimension of existence wherein the essential condition of things exists in an imminent relationship. Thus, it is through immediate cognition, from the perspective of the human singularity, that we discover the nature of the incorporeal dimension of existence.

11. The Corporeal Faculties

Prerequisite to the practice of immediate cognition is the determination to engage things as they exist originally, without presumption or interpretation of any kind. Thus, when we engage phenomena elementally we thereby avoid the conventional practices of association because we encounter things from a straightforward perspective. Therefore, our conclusions will be all the more profound because of the insight that we gain from an unalloyed, unambiguous approach.

The word *being* implies an existing condition which continues when all transient bodily properties and faculties are inhibited. Moreover, by inhibition, we gain autonomy over the application of cognitive powers. Thus, conscious of the distinction between the essential human being and the capacity to process information, it becomes clear that thought as we understand it, must not be confused with being. In fact, we do not intrinsically own the ability to reflect and deliberate, we merely use it as part of the corporeal constitution.

Thus, for example, the essential human being is inherently able to distinguish one person from another irrespective of their physical appearance because it exists elementally and sees things profoundly. Consequently, the individual singular distinction of existence possesses the capacity to engage phenomena uniquely through direct experience. Clearly, the difference between conventional, abstractly influenced thinking and the immediate encounter of a phenomenon from the essential perspective, necessarily rests upon the purity of observation.

If we encounter circumstances from a pre-established position founded upon prior experience and antecedent conclusions, we hinder the possibility of original engagement and rely heavily upon vested interpretation. However, the essential identity that is the unique singularity of every human being, always sees the fundamental of things because it does not depend upon the corporeal, evaluative faculties. In other words, the distinction between oblique evaluation and immediate engagement also rests upon the directness of approach.

We recognize the intrinsic human identity when we withhold our conventional cognitive practices and when calculation, association, and feeling assessment are stilled. In the silence, we directly discern our unique distinction of existence. Recognizing respective singularity, the observer establishes a cognitive perspective towards other things from the position of our own directly engaged identity. Thus, everything is experienced essentially because we encounter phenomena straightforwardly and unconditionally, without the intrusion of conventional cognitive practices. Consequently, without relying on past experience, associative evaluation and preferential prejudices, things are recognized as they exist in their own right.

Through immediacy, the human essence encounters phenomena as they are substantively and not as we assume or deduce them to be. Similarly, the condition wherein we find circumstances as they exist independently of our evaluation and pre-conceptual assessment, is immanent and inherently profound. Furthermore, the volume wherein the intrinsic significance of things resides exists independently of physical coordinates.

Therefore, the discovery of the independent condition of the existence of something requires the straightforward engagement of the human entity. Only the intrinsic person can directly encounter a phenomenon. The intellect operates indirectly serving the human being as a corporeal function. Therefore, we see that without intrinsic identity, immediate engagement would be impossible and the human being would be condemned to obliquely functioning speculation. Fortunately, this scenario is not the reality.

However, although we recognize the existence of an intrinsic volume of existence through the practice of immediate cognition, the establishment of the human entity as the sovereign identity of the human being is hindered by an obsolete mentality and ethos. Consequently, egocentricity confuses and preoccupies us, and bedeviled by protracted, emotional restlessness established upon an uncertain psychology, we remain confined within the shortcomings of an unsuitable mentality, irrespective of profound insights.

The sad fact is that predominantly, humanity is existentially insecure and rough-hewn. Consequently, a suitable ethos must become installed in order to ensure a truly meaningful future. Fortunately and predictably, life has installed a paragon of the ideal character and disposition contiguously positioned at the human heart. Of necessity, identification with the supernal nature is a vital step in terms of the qualitative transformation of the soul.

The state of insufficiency of the human soul is self-evident not only through an examination of extreme examples, but it is apparent wherever unease and discomposure erupt and propagate. Typically, agitation and imbalance occur not exceptionally but all too frequently, while the subsequent commotion is accepted by convention as tolerable unless it becomes acute. Thus, we often find ourselves impelled and goaded to react defensively and inappropriately through the disquiet of a redundant, emotional predisposition. But it need not be this way.

Thereupon, we discover that the heart of the human soul is the place wherein a successive disposition must be inaugurated. We are well aware of the tenacious nature of the redundant mentality that impedes further development, and we recognize the necessity of extrinsic intervention. At this decisive moment of realization, through sincere open-heartedness, the individual soul discovers the presence of an exemplary nature and we find that, like all intangible distinctions, the supernal ethos is imminently apparent.

Intriguingly, the presence of an exemplary nature is analogous to the biblical *still, small voice*. However, the ancient instruction is incomplete because the human heart, in this case, is not only the organ of perception, but the place where the transformation of the soul must take place. That is, the heart must become receptively prepared in order that an essential communion with the supernal nature may take place.

The capricious and petty human soul is obsolete in terms of meaningful advancement and does not possess the capacity of self-reestablishment. But unless it is transformed it will forever impede the development of individual sovereign autonomy. Therefore, in order that the soul may become beneficially reestablished, each person must open the heart towards restoration. The supernal nature is immanent and therefore it merely requires an open heart and a vulnerable mien to inaugurate the transformative process of dispositional reorientation. The establishment of a new character therefore, becomes a very feasible undertaking, accessible to every person who wholeheartedly desires to embark upon this most remarkable adventure of all.

We cannot know what that future condition is, but we intimate that it is quite unlike the mess we have got ourselves into which is the source of extensive human misery on the large scale and personal disquiet among even the most fortunate. The development of character and demeanor of an exemplary caliber, qualitatively alike to the supernal ethos of integrity and goodwill cannot be neglected because our present insufficient mentality will otherwise always pull us contrarily every which way, whether we desire it or not.

The supernal reestablishes the human soul through the direct influence of its own nature to the degree of the receptivity of the human heart, because it is within the heart that character is conceived for good or ill. In other words, an affinity of heart towards the exemplary disposition naturally furthers the transformation of the psyche.

The qualitative nature of the immanent presence is discovered through direct encounter, and in retrospect, from the resulting amendments that occur within the heart of the soul. But the individual must approach these things with an open heart and a vulnerable mien, even though the transformative events themselves are beyond our capacity to influence because the supernal ethos is not of human conception.

Furthermore, it is unnecessary and even counter-productive to become excessively religiously preoccupied if doctrine and ritual readily become a substitute for the authentic experience. In other words, we are not interested in the counterfeit because it is an aspect of the obsolete mentality that we desire to supersede. But, fortunately, the successive dispositional paradigm is initiated only through sincerity because thereby the heart is appropriately conditioned towards essential reorientation.

12. The Intellectual Approach

In order to discover the manner in which things exist profoundly, we must leave both intellectuality and feeling evaluation temporarily behind in order to engage circumstances directly. Then we understand life and discover the deeper purpose. But preoccupation with deduction and scholarship, abstract evaluation and the emotional perspective, is a significant impediment to immediate cognition because the abstract view seems to suggest a sufficiency of existential understanding where, in fact, there is very little. Naively, one wonders what more there could be beyond intellectual acumen. But that is entirely the wrong end of the stick.

But immediate cognition is our destined cognitive approach in terms of elemental knowledge because it is not an act of appraisal but a view that offers an entirely definitive experience of a situation. The intellect should not supersede it in terms of understanding existence, but, nevertheless, abstract thinking can serve humanity in the many ways that research and invention does now. Therefore, the present conceptual approach is tempered when we recognize the profound essential conditions of existence. This is the ideal strategy because it advances human perception beyond oblique rationale and subjective estimation to discover things in their actual condition of existence through straightforward engagement.

In this way, we recognize the importance of two other very considerable approaches that are essential towards the fulfillment of a well-balanced human autonomy. The first is directly derived knowledge concerning elemental conditions. This expands our view dimensionally because it demonstrates how things are when we look further than merely the obvious material conditions of existence. Thus, it gives human experience meaning and purpose and a foundational premise to our understanding that is emphatically real. In fact, it lends irrefutable evidence to the existence of an immanent and substantive underlying foundation.

The second standpoint concerns the human ethos. At present, the *do unto others,* golden rule is often the best we can hope for. But if the other person is deceitful, then we will necessarily abandon that maxim because, in practice, it is insufficient and naive. How much more effective is the actual development of our own human disposition in harmony with the supernal nature? Indeed, we will find, as we practice openhearted sincerity, that circumstances in our lives and relationships undergo a pivotal shift towards qualitative betterment.

Thus, in terms of things as they are now, the necessity of an immediate, cognitive experience of the human intrinsic distinction is pivotal to the development of straightforward engagement. The singular distinction of every human being must become the ultimate perspective from which we engage phenomena in order that we may discover things, not as we surmise them to be, but as they actually exist. Thereby, human understanding will rest upon a solid existential basis.

At first, when the nature of human identity is conceptually considered and reasoned abstractly, we naturally associate our existence with conditions which are already familiar. We inevitably conclude that the physically elusive is merely subjectively identified since the body appears to be our most obvious identity. This is because we assume that there are only two cognitive approaches. The first is detached and impartial, while the subjective stance merely offers indecisive intelligence. But immediate cognition from the essential perspective remains at this time, very improperly explored.

But in reality, the detached, deductive approach towards phenomena is ultimately unable to achieve a conclusive evaluation unless the components are quantifiably reducible. As we have argued, reason cannot experience because it is a corporeal function and not an entity. Only the human, intrinsic distinction of existence is able to engage the phenomena directly and discover the extant condition of their existence. Consequently, compared to immediate cognition, definitive, existential knowledge through detached, intellectual evaluation is little more that a myth because rationale is an indirectly operating function, and consequently, it cannot evaluate the fundamental conditions of circumstances. This realization, of itself, should prompt us to search for a more direct and profound way of thinking.

Thus, when the manner of inquiry moves away from constricted interpretive evaluation and assessment based upon our feelings, and becomes established upon the insight of the human, intrinsic distinction then the experience becomes both immediate and decisive. It is no longer evaluative, because it is not the intellect or the feelings that know the essential value of something, but the human identity itself that immediately discovers the inherent significance.

Thus, we recognize that the human, intrinsic distinction does not rely on subjective evaluation, but engages phenomena directly, without intermediary interpretation. However, the conventional cognitive approaches of deduction and subjective evaluation cannot grasp the significance of a human condition that exists independently of the body because incorporeality cannot be assessed in the conventional, cognitive manner. Thus, the dismissal of the significance of intangible merit merely rests upon prejudicial preference.

Those who recognize and are willing to explore the significance of their own singular distinction of existence will discover that the essential identity of the human being resides within a condition of immediacy and permanence. On this basis, we are much encouraged. But we must still do something about the obvious shortcoming of the human mentality. Obviously, there is no meaningful future while humanity lurches from one self-made catastrophe to the next, and if we cannot control our passions because the petty sense of self cares little for anyone else but itself, all the insight in the world will not make up the deficit.

Therefore, human uprightness and goodwill must also be addressed. And, indeed, as we have described, there is a way forward towards an improved ethos in that area as well. Fortunately, the actual transformation of the quality and character of the soul is not achieved by human resources. Our task is to position ourselves appropriately through sincerity, and permit supernal ingress to influence the deepest recesses of the heart whereupon the necessary transformation may be inaugurated and accomplished. Always remembering, of course, that this is an individual and personal journey that none can make for us.

13. Egocentricity and Defensiveness

As we reiterated in the previous chapter, we cannot arrive at a conclusive appreciation of intangible significances if we rely upon accumulated scholarship and inevitable, historical embellishment. But we can develop a cognitive practice that engages physical phenomena directly and which subsequently reveals the overlooked, qualitative dimension of things and their elemental integrity.

In order to discern the manner in which things exist elementally, we must leave behind both preconception and feeling evaluation in order to engage circumstances directly. That is, in order to allow things to reveal what they are, we must engage them without preconceived assessment. Or, to put the situation another way, the qualitative nature of something is not the same as the obvious physical properties. The former exists intrinsically and deals with the identity, while the physical concerns surface conditions.

The intrinsic identity of something is the intangible elemental condition. It is the essential identification or substantive nomen. Thus, when we observe, and permit things to be as they are, and resist the common tendency to classify phenomena on the strength of their appearance, we begin to recognize unique and concise entities. We recognize them according to their nature and the particular expression of their existence.

In terms of the human being, through immediacy, we experientially recognize the absolute reality of our own singular existence and, subsequently, we regard the corporeal appearance as superficial because we discover that our physical status is not our intrinsic identity. Further, we find that we cannot identify our unique distinction with the body or any of its functions. But through straightforward experience and observation from a pure unsullied perspective, we discover that we possess intrinsic distinction. Also, we know that the intellect cannot evaluate the existence of the human essence because deduction is a corporeal function, and a faculty is incapable of immediate experience.

We find that when we encounter other people from the position of our sovereign existence; we recognize their similarly singular uniqueness. Additionally, when the human essence directly engages phenomena, as described above, the elemental condition of the existence of things is also discovered as the intrinsic significance. Thus, through immediate cognition from the perspective of the human, essential distinction, the substantive value of things is discerned to exist in a condition of immediacy and intangibility. In other words, essential existences reside only in an immediate condition and remain elusive to indirect evaluation.

The emancipation and further qualitative development of the human soul, for the most part, remains beyond the influence of the practice of immediate cognition. That is to say, we cannot significantly and lastingly improve human character on the strength of insight through immediate cognition. But convincing knowledge concerning essential immanent conditions by one's own research encourages the individual to explore the efficacy of dispositional transformation through the agency of openhearted sincerity.

Egotism founded upon existential uncertainty, and anxiety intrudes upon the immediate discovery of the essential existence of things. Further, we find that trenchant insecurity and its subsequent defensiveness is not amended merely through behavioral adjustments or doctrinal adherence. Therefore, the human soul cannot realistically, qualitatively advance until the moribund mentality is superseded by an appropriately suitable ethos.

At present, the human soul remains very poorly equipped for a destiny of existential and cognitive autonomy. We may wish to collaborate towards our betterment and not to detract, but the obsolete mentality that we have established hinders real progress. In other words, we are predisposed to defensiveness and egocentric preservation, but clearly there is no meaningful future for a mindset established upon self-first. Thus, humanity remains in a kind of limbo, fearful of further calamity.

It is essential that the foundation of the human soul, formerly established upon a trivial sense of self, be fundamentally reconstituted in terms that are appropriate to a meaningful and autonomous future. But we do not possess the means whereby a pertinent mentality and disposition may replace obsolete uncertainty and defensiveness. Nevertheless, a distinctly contrasting ethos is urgently required.

We recognize the manner of the imminent existence of the essential condition of things because we have discovered the intrinsic dimension directly, through immediate cognition. In order to do so, we had to restrain assumption and supposition.

In the same way, it is important to set aside pre-established notions and concepts and, through openhearted sincerity, allow the supernal to remain unembellished by preconceptions. Thereby, those things that we cannot envisage are not distorted to resemble something fictional and humanly conceived.

We are well aware of the over-confidence of religious authority and the pretension of messianism, and we recognize the failure of those initiatives and contrivances. To follow such teachings blindly will detract from our own progress if we neglect the priority of the individual quest. Thus, we approach the immanent presence directly, unconditionally, without pre-established expectation, and thereupon we silently attend in sincere and openhearted communion, allowing supernal integrity and goodwill to effect our improvement.

The pious will prostrate themselves as if before a human authority and cajole for imagined advantage. It is supposed that a deity can be persuaded to intercede with circumstances on behalf of the petitioner if certain practices are strictly followed. This is tantamount to magic and entirely remote from our purpose because we are endeavoring qualitatively to transform the human mentality, but not to practice vodoun.

In reality, the human soul of itself cannot develop according to the supernal disposition unless the heart directly experiences the exemplary nature. However, through openhearted sincerity, we allow ourselves to be cherished and all others to be similarly beloved. Thereby, the qualitative development of the soul is committed to a vastly higher wisdom than our own.

If we return to the parallel of immediate cognition,

that which we desire is knowledge of the way things actually are. In a similar manner, we wish our experience of the supernal nature to be authentic in every respect. It is for this reason that we restrain human preconception and contrived interpretation. Already, centuries of religiously inspired mayhem and cruelty have demonstrated how the devout can turn against one another and virtue can be quickly transformed into hatred.

Openhearted sincerity enables the individual to directly and experientially discern the existence of the supernal nature. From our exploration of immediate cognition, we have developed a mindfulness of elemental conditions through our personal practice. Consequently, we are aware of the qualitative timbre of essential existence, and we cannot be easily deceived. That is, we know what essential conditions are like and from our own experience, we can determine the real from the counterfeit. Therefore, when we engage a phenomenon immediately from the perspective of our essential existence, we necessarily discover things as they inherently are. We have set aside professed knowledge in order that we may encounter phenomena straightforwardly. And it is the same with matters concerning communion with the supernal nature through the heart of the soul.

In other words, immediately, when we recognize our extant uniqueness, which is our authentic distinction, we establish an infallible point of view. From the perspective of the singular human significance, we cease to rely upon oblique evaluation and subjective assessment and, consequently, we can engage things in their essential condition. Consequently, every occasion whereupon we engage the intrinsic state of the existence of something, is a moment of immediate, experiential cognition concerning reality. Thus, a direct encounter with the authentic state of something is not only a qualitative benchmark against which we can compare contrived conceptualizations for their substance, but also a cognitive experience of the full existential dimension of things.

The condition of reality discovered through the straightforward engagement of the human quintessence is the state wherein everything is apprehended for its authentic identity. It is an extraordinary condition only by virtue of our unfamiliarity because we imagine that we already know what reality is based upon the entrench nature of material philosophy.

Those who claim the authority of religious orthodoxy and metaphysical scholarship frequently assume a determined monopoly over what constitutes reality. Thereby, they readily disregard the significance of that which is beyond the scope of their convictions and assume that contradiction is merely sectarian and without merit if it seems remote from the familiar point of view that they espouse. But the conventional manner of thinking that we rely upon is incommensurate with immediate cognition and incapable of properly evaluating the results of the direct encounter.

We wish to know the authentic nature and the intrinsic condition of the existence of things. In order to accomplish this, we must allow essential circumstances to remain as they are without the intrusive interference of human conjecture and the time wasting application of incompatible assessment.

Immediacy is the physically elusive dimension of elemental existence. Similarly, within the immediacy of the human heart, we discover the supernal ethos through direct engagement. It is this directly experienced nature that we yearn to emulate and establish as a successive dispositional mien instead of our familiar impoverished mentality. Through sincerity and open-hearted communion, this hope is steadily realized.

14. Dimensionality

When the full significance of a phenomenon is discovered through immediate cognition, both the object of perception and the human intrinsic distinction of existence, through the straightforwardness of the approach, are found to occupy the condition that is experientially recognized as immediacy. Compared with a materialistic preoccupation with the physical appearance of things and the oblique practice of evaluation that tries to reason the nature of existence upon the basis of exclusively material evidence, human immediate cognition inevitably is the vastly more significant approach. Thereby, the substantive and intrinsic condition of the existence of things is found to be of greater relevance than the three-dimensional appearances because it concerns the fundamental nature of the distinction of things.

The direct experience of the immanent volume reveals a depth which inspires the human soul towards a similar expansion and a desire to maintain this perspective. Furthermore, immediate cognition provides certain substantive existential evidence, that is, nonetheless, always anchored to the physical. In this way navigation of the elemental world is always securely supported.

This demonstrates an important distinction between mysticism and immediate cognition. The mystical experience is capricious, and the sage must guess in a haphazard way at the meaning of unattached and perplexing intuition that is often heavily influenced emotionally. But by immediate cognition, observation is securely established upon the familiar physical. The observer merely grasps the nature of the elemental condition of already commonplace circumstances.

Similarly, in terms of the human heart as an approach to the supernal nature, the individual uses openhearted sincerity as a reference, and communion with the ideal principle remains securely within those parameters. It is an interchange that requires complete receptivity, whereupon, as a newborn, we allow the soul to become refashioned according to the influence of the supernal disposition.

It is supposed by many that human nature cannot change and, indeed, if the present mentality remains limited by materialism and consumed as if the superficial were the full extent of existence, there would be little hope of improvement. Even sweeping technological advancements that suggest human progress remain empty because they concern only outward circumstances and do not necessarily influence the dire predicament that is the human plight.

Consequently, we need to know how the maturation and reorientation of the human soul may be accomplished in order that we may individually qualitatively advance towards a sound mind and a disposition of goodwill that is commensurate with our better angels.

The distinction between immediate cognition and conventional assessment through an exclusive scrutiny of the physical dimension of phenomena is indicative of the shallow view as opposed to the profound. Consequently, the human soul must become similarly, profoundly reestablished in order that which we say and do may be worthwhile and purposefully productive. Therefore, the heart must embrace an appropriate ethos that anticipates a fruitful life of significance and creativity.

But this cannot be accomplished through human agency alone because we need to establish a quintessentially refashioned psyche at the most fundamental level. That is to say, a wound-dressing of the thinking and feeling, or reliance upon medication, may offer positive remediation in a piece-meal temporary fashion but they will not impact the human mentality as a whole and the treatment will have to be endlessly repeated.

In other words, the human being is tragic, and it is no wonder that we travail under myriad incomprehensible adversities when our perspective is skewed and our mentality is petty. But it need not remain that way because contrary to the way things seem, the narrow view is not the full extent of existence and the psychical constitution can become reestablished through the direct influence of the supernal nature upon the heart.

Furthermore, through openhearted sincerity and willingness, the individual soul will begin to become reinstated according to meaningful coordinates. Indeed, through a receptive mien, we initiate a process of steady qualitative advancement and thereby abandon the constraints of the former moribund mentality that immobilizes human potential and a worthwhile destiny.

At present, not only is genuine human identity slandered under the assumption of bodily misidentification, but the soul itself has degenerated into existential ignorance, and from innocence to deceit. We have become adrift and disoriented. That which is important, we overlook while the trivial preoccupies our attention. Consequently, while immediate cognition can reestablish perspective, openhearted sincerity towards the immanent supernal nature remains unavoidably crucial in terms of reorientation and the urgent priority of a sound ethos.

15. Transformation

Popular, human identification with the animal kingdom only exacerbates a materialistic perspective because it implies that the extent of human destiny will always remain essentially animalian. Indeed, if we deny the existence of the human, incorporeal distinction, we condemn ourselves to the status of the creature.

However, through immediate cognition, we look more profoundly at the obvious, physical appearance of things and encounter the intrinsic substance or elemental condition that is the most fundamental existential condition. Similarly, from the perspective of our unique distinction, we discover the singular identity of ourselves and others. We quickly recognize that human beings are not all identical and merely physically differentiated through small corporeal variances, but that we are inherently distinct. It is the inherent distinction which is the genuine, unique and singular identity of the human being, not the external body.

Similarly, all phenomena can be either superficially evaluated or discerned on the basis of the substantiality of their existence. It is this essential manner of cognition that we desire to consistently sustain because it enables us to determine the authentic condition of things and to exist in a condition wherein everything is profoundly revealed.

Through considerable practice, we may increasingly discover the volume of inherent existence by means of immediate engagement and recognize our own intrinsic significance and that of others. Nevertheless, the moribund condition of the human mentality remains an obstructive precedent because it rests upon obsolete but deeply rooted misapprehensions. In order that we may steadfastly maintain our singular distinction as the sovereign seat of our existence, we must address the disturbing and detrimental manner in which we habitually relate to one another and confront challenging circumstances with wisdom.

Consequently, human nature must change because, as it stands, for the most part, the human psyche is self-defeating and the acceptable standard of decency is not established upon principle but through compromise. Perhaps it was appropriate for an old era of crude survival, but egoism and defensiveness are certainly redundant in terms of our qualitative advancement.

An impressive canon of scholarly erudition and imaginative rationale exists concerning the reestablishment of the human soul upon a meaningful and productive course. However, it appears as if only a religious and philosophical elite possesses the requisite knowledge concerning human advancement while the scientific and psychological schools, through antithetical conviction, insist that the prerogative is exclusively their own.

However, the progress of the human being towards a destiny of sovereign autonomy remains completely at the discretion of each person. This is not the sole prerogative of the clerical elite or the philosopher, but the responsibility of the respective individual. It requires that the individual inaugurates the process and maintains the momentum. And no one else can do it for us because the development of the human soul requires active personal participation.

The human soul, under the aegis of conscience and disquiet is well aware of the shortcomings of a habitually reactive approach to circumstances. But we do not possess within ourselves the capacity of self-amelioration. By concerted determination, we can adjust some behaviors to a small extent. But not deficiencies of character, compulsions and our congenital dysfunctions. These things are too deeply seated.

But through the heart, the human soul is able to embrace a dynamic whereby the former, obsolete mentality is transformed into a disposition founded not upon apprehension and defensiveness but existential assurance and peace. While the means of redress do not reside within our own constitution, nevertheless healing is immediately available through the human heart. Thus, the soul may be transformed through the amity of immanent, goodwill by the establishment of active communion.

In matters that concern personal development there is little value in the mere abstract acceptance of a concept because necessarily, we must be personally proactive or our disposition will not improve one iota. The dynamic of transformation involves our own essential selves, and we should not imagine that a complete reorientation is accomplished without our intimate involvement. Change must be applied, pragmatic and apparent. It must actually occur and not be merely hoped for or imagined in order for the soul to advance. It is absurd to assume that we can establish a position of existential confidence and consolidate character amelioration through passivity or on the whim of miraculous, divine clemency.

The opportunity of transformation of the human soul occurs through the experience of life itself. Commonplace events present both challenge and opportunity. Small but noticeable ironies intrude upon the moment as productive alternatives and it is our task to be attentive to their occurrence because they alert us to an entirely different perspective which, if pursued, offers an extraordinary opportunity of transformational enriching. But, in order to completely reconstruct the human psychical constitution, we cannot do without a close heavenly relationship.

Nevertheless, to reiterate, the soul is not reconstructed through heavenly magic. If that were so, we would have to relinquish our potential autonomy. But the supernal provides existential and emotional security through immediate access to the divine exemplar. Our role is to reach full agreement within the heart. This is what educates and changes the psyche. Thus, a better approach is indicated than our classic reactive attitude which, if fully acknowledged, modifies both perspective and disposition. Consequently, through an increasing alertness to irony and paradox, and attention to conscience, we become alert towards opportunities to adopt a different perspective from our conventional, egotistical custom.

In other words, after a distressful situation, the conscience reveals the insufficiency of the familiar way of handling a situation, and we subsequently approach the supernal nature through openhearted sincerity. Through insight concerning a more comprehensive perspective, a determination is established within us as a grain of resolve. Thereupon, a change occurs. The timbre of our individual nature improves. That which we assumed to be the temper of our personality is transformed because contrition, inevitably, alters the tenor of the soul. Further, encouragement in this way makes us alert towards inevitable, subsequent opportunities.

Thus, the human soul, eager for its own transformation, opens the heart to immanent goodwill and through sincerity, a concurrence is established whereby the individual is prepared through willingness for its own instruction. Consequently, we anticipate the opportunities of choice that we recognize through moments of conscience and steadily we become familiar with the methodology. In other words, there is a better way of looking at things, and, accordingly, the immanent presence inspires the receptive heart not only to see with understanding but to be an effectively better person.

A simple sketch may help to illustrate the dynamic of soul transformation. We enter the supernal presence through openhearted sincerity, and thereby we become aware of a greater perspective of amity and goodwill through immediate experience. In other words, we actually live it in our hearts. Consequently, we find ourselves both consoled and fortified, and appropriately resolved.

If a situation arises in our lives where we find ourselves defensive and impatient, and lose all perspective through agitation, we know what to do. Turning the heart towards imminent wisdom, we become aware of an alternative perspective, and we are struck with both the poignancy of the situation and remorse. Indeed, it is as if we were reenacting a situation while also observing. Thereby, we experience the catharsis of profound remorse.

The same dynamic is recognized as instrumental to the forgiveness of others. Through the amity and security that we experience by means of openhearted sincerity towards the supernal nature, we engage the offender in our hearts and find ourselves desirous of goodwill because the situation is revealed from the greater supernal perspective. Thereby, we relinquish both resentment and defensiveness because we now see things insightfully. In this sense, both parties are absolved.

But because this occurs within the heart and in the supernal presence, the nature of the individual changes, and consequently, all other things alter for the better. That is to say, when human nature undergoes profound betterment, the quality of life itself improves.

16. Sincerity

We necessarily enter an area of great uncertainty when we seek to encounter intangible significances that are entirely unrepresented through physical references. Nevertheless, based upon the immediate cognition of the intrinsic condition of phenomena we are well aware of the existence of an intangible dimension to existence.

Thus, we explore elemental significances such as the intangibly extant distinction of a color that retains its consistent identity wherever it may happen to arise. Similarly, we recognize the essential condition of a Native Element Mineral and find that its intrinsic distinction lies in its intangible significance and not solely with the physically obvious appearance and properties.

Furthermore, through the immediate engagement of the human ipseity with a physical phenomenon, we discover both conceptual origin and volition in much the same manner as we would justify the appearance of a humanly conceived and manufactured item. Likewise, the commonalities of organization and function between creatures reveal archetypal conceptualization; While the manner whereby they pursue a distinct and consistent cycle of metamorphic development indicates volition. Moreover, the disparities of expression reveal particular qualitative distinctions that are intangible, although the consequences are readily evident through physical variety.

Of crucial significance to the development of the human capacity of immediate engagement, is the recognition of our own unique distinction of existence that resides inherently and possesses only superficial, physical representation. It is through the ipseity of our existence that we are able to discover the similarly unique and intransigent distinction of all other things.

Thus, a vast dimension of intangible significance becomes recognizable that is of far greater consequence than the material condition because while the essential influences the carapace, the essence of a thing does not exist superficially. That is, elemental conditions reside intrinsically as the qualitative nature of the existence of something. But it is the fundamental and elemental significance of phenomena that reveals their authentic identity and not the transient appearance. Furthermore, we recognize that the essential exists in an imminent condition to our own profound distinction. It is for this reason that we are able to discern the intrinsic significance of things, because we view them from our own essential perspective.

However, the human soul, unlike the ipseity, is established upon an archaic mentality that is insufficient for a meaningful future. But a marked distinction exists between the individual quintessence and the temperamental disposition. The former is the human, intrinsic existence that remains an incorruptible fact of being while, our disposition involves the qualitative tenor of the human being.

The intellect cannot effectively address or cure emotional dysfunction because, while reason may sway the heart, a cathartic event requires extraordinary profundity in order to transform character.. Similarly, while the immediate experience of elemental significances reveals the authenticity of an intangible dimension of existence, emotional uncertainties are only temporarily assuaged through direct cognition. Consequently, a lasting transformation of the soul is not humanly attainable, but requires a wisdom and perspective beyond our limited capacities.

We discover the supernal nature through the same direct approach whereby we discern the intrinsic distinction of all phenomena. However, in terms of the soul, the open heart is the portal of psychical transformation.

Through the immediate engagement of the heart, we find an exemplary nature contiguously positioned before the soul itself. It resides as both a solace against the absurdity of egocentricity and defensiveness, and as a refuge from our redundant disposition and narrow, self-circumscribed perspective. Continually, as the conscience reveals an unworkable stance or behavior, we turn towards the immanent principle and steadily, the constitution of our soul is reconstituted. Therefore, through retrospect, we recognize the progress of qualitative transformation. Obviously, we cannot anticipate the nature of the reconstructed soul, but we recognize that our successive disposition is entirely unlike our former mentality.

From a conventional point of view, it would seem strange that the heart should serve as a channel between the soul and the immanent principle. But we need not be surprised. It is similarly through the heart that an innocent child learns from its parents. Thus, in refashioning the human mentality all over again upon a vastly more noble basis, the heart is the obvious instrument because it is there that the original nature was established, for good or ill. However, this time, our education is conscious, and the mentor is the supernal nature itself.

In other words, the transformation is not accomplished through our own merit, but, by a combination of vulnerability and subsequent receptivity, an entirely new condition is inaugurated within the soul that is not of our making. The human heart is opened in order that improvement may be steadily consummated. This requires sincerity and diligence, but we are severely mistaken if we imagine that we are capable of achieving qualitative restoration by ourselves. We have no idea of our subsequent nature, nor of the means of its realization, nevertheless, with the first attempt, we become convinced.

Supernal goodwill makes our destiny secure by reestablishing our soul once and for all upon the secure foundation of a sound ethos, replacing former enmity and uncertainty with existential confidence, to the degree that we permit the transformation.

Thus, the dynamic of soul transformation, whereby the qualitative exemplar of the supernal nature becomes established as a foundational condition of the human soul, is discovered to exist as a substantial reality. The heart opens to the immediacy of goodwill, which resides neither within nor without physical parameters, but imminently.

This seems a considerable stretch to the materialist who has no basis of understanding physically elusive conditions. But we must consider that qualities such as goodwill, wisdom or sincerity exist as authentically as concrete, yet they are completely metaphysical.

If phenomena were open-mindedly explored

through observation and direct engagement, the significance of intrinsic, qualitative distinctions would be self-evident. But the materialist traces all consciousness to brain function because that is the sole physical organ that can be attributed with thought. Similarly, brain activity is associated with biochemical, electrical or physical stimulus and the human being is thereby reduced to a common automaton without intrinsic individuality.

However, experientially, we notice that when the soul immediately experiences the heavenly nature in the heart; we recognize goodwill through directly verified evidence. That is to say, the intrinsic feelings become an organ of dialog between the human soul and the supernal exemplar. Thus, no belief or faith is necessary because we know the efficacy of openhearted sincerity first hand.

Immediacy will be discussed further in the next chapter. This is a difficult concept to grasp until the essential dimension of phenomena is personally lived by direct cognition. However, through the heart, an impending coincidence is established that replaces our earlier convictions with profound and meaningful assurance. In this way, we also discover through greater insight the intrinsic context of circumstances.

17. Immediacy

Similar to the manner whereby we determine the intrinsic significance of a phenomenon, the singular distinction of ourselves or of someone else, we must restrain the conventional practices of intellectual presumption and emotional evaluation in order to also recognize immediately how physical coordinates are involved. Thus, by preemptive inhibition we encounter material conditions from an existentially profound perspective that is immediate, and from that point of view we recognize that the essential substance of all things exists uninfluenced by the nominal counterpart.

The nominal counterpart might be described as the carapace or physical shell. Or, using a grammatical analogy, the material condition can be represented as the noun, while the qualifiers reside within a different context that is without physical dimension and exist immediately. Describing these things in this way, it becomes clear that an entirely different approach is required than that used to understand the physical. Indeed, we enter into the province of the fine artist. In order to describe elusive conditions, we require the subtle terminology of figurative and metaphorical expression.

Thus, we recognize that an exchange that occurs solely in the heart of the human being is an experience that is physically remote. Indeed, it is an immediate event. It is for this reason that the materialist balks. An entrenched exclusively concrete philosophy has been established that overrides what is essentially very straightforward but subtle. This would matter less if this was merely touted as an opinion, but materialism has become a determined way of looking at life. Yet, balanced with common sense, clearly materialistic philosophy is a narrow abstraction far remove from reality.

Thus, we recognize, and can more easily accept, that resident within the constitution of the human psyche exists the potential of soul rehabilitation. Through the guidance and goodwill of an entity of absolute integrity, the stature of whom is beyond the capacities of our conventional abilities and our habitual cognitional approach to grasp, these things become possible. Therefore, by active susceptibility, we relinquish our obsolete mentality and we identify with the perspective of the supernal nature as if it were our own.

Steadily, to the degree that we directly engage the supernal through the conduit of the human heart, our disposition is reestablished upon the sound footing of comprehensive assurance. We recognize that our best attempts to accommodate our uncertain psyche pale beside immanent wisdom and goodwill. Consequently, it is through a forthright concourse within the human heart and not through emotional evaluation or intellectual deduction, that we glimpse the possibility of a mature successive disposition.

We find this a very exciting prospect because if direct concurrence within the human soul were not authentic the consequences would be dire indeed. The human being would remain trapped in a condition of existential ignorance compounded by an ethical insufficiency. We would seek respite through all physical and imaginable means and find no permanent sustenance or viable recourse. We would remain preoccupied within an insubstantial and narrow perspective towards existence, condemned through the shortcomings of an obsolete, self-circumscribed condition of soul founded upon uncertainty and anxiety.

In summary, through immediate experience, without precondition and suppositional bias, we discover that we possess a uniquely singular distinction of existence. Further, we find that through the uniqueness of the human ipseity we are able to discern the intrinsic condition of phenomena. Consequently, by the same means of forthright, untarnished immediacy, we similarly discover that there exists, imminently available to us as a remedy for those awful conditions described above, a corrective that only awaits our sincere willingness.

To describe the supernal nature in anything except general terms, establishes a pre-conceptual assumption between the soul and immediate, unbiased experience and, thereby, we may imagine that we comprehend the situation instead of discovering its nature through direct and personal experience. In other words, the way forward is not accomplished upon the strength of supposed knowledge and philosophical concurrence, but requires that every individual discover the transformational process for themselves.

Neither do we imagine and formulate a solution or remedy to our redundant condition of soul. This would be entirely counterproductive because it is not our own way or perspective that we wish to implement. We have already attempted self-improvement to no permanent avail. But on the contrary, it is necessary to assume a condition of attentive receptivity in order that we may advance because, compared with the direct perspective of the exemplary nature, we recognize that we know nothing.

Indeed, if we already possessed the explication and knowledge of our potential, and if we were fully aware of the ameliorated state that is essential to the unfolding of a meaningful destiny, there would be a tremendous incentive to explore openhearted sincerity. But the soul of a child is a blank sheet, and straightforwardness must be our own approach.

However, the assumption that we can, through reason and scholarship, comprehend something that we know nothing about is one of the fallacies of traditional religious authority that rob us of both our personal commission and all subsequent hope of authentic existential autonomy. Assumption of knowledge that we do not possess is precisely the mindset that works against us. It is blatantly obvious wherever we turn our gaze, that we are woefully ignorant of matters pertaining to the qualitative betterment of the human soul. Nevertheless, it is a wonderful thing to admit ignorance because thereby we may learn something otherwise unexplored.

We approach the imminent presence through the heart, but we do not imagine for a second that we are able to reconstitute our own soul. We do not want what we conceive to be a refashioned mentality. There is neither value nor satisfaction in becoming the way we imagine an emancipated soul should be. Self-righteousness and puritanism, fanaticism and doctrinal zealotry are the almost inevitable consequence if we pursue our own understanding of what constitutes completeness.

Indeed, if we assume that we can discover all that is to be known through our conventional, cognitive faculties of reason and scholarship or through feeling determination, we commence our exploration upon an entirely erroneous footing. Similarly, if we imagine that we already possess adequate knowledge concerning the exemplary nature and the dynamic of soul transformation through open-hearted sincerity, then the authentic experience will remain remote to us. It is as if we were to ask a traveler to describe a foreign land that we ourselves have never visited, but instead, we proceed to characterize the place based upon our academic intelligence and completely ignore the traveler's firsthand experience.

We possess very little real knowledge concerning the supernal nor can we truly know much about the transformative dynamic of the soul except through immediate experience. That is to say, in the light of exceptional, directly ascertained comprehension our entire, hypothetical understanding is worthless.

To quote St. Thomas Aquinas (1225-1274) *The end of my labors has come. All that I have written appears to be as so much straw after the things that have been revealed. I can write no more.*

18. Active Participation

When the human soul is transformed to a sound mind and an outstanding ethos, and securely established through the aegis and immediacy of supernal goodwill, the ipseity that is the essential human distinction, is able to engage phenomena directly without the impediment of a distracted mentality. The ipseity and the emancipated soul coincide and thereby fashion an extraordinary human being with autonomous distinction. A soul, akin in stature and rectitude to that of the exemplary nature, becomes a certainty as the metamorphosis of the human psyche is progressively accomplished and a completed human being emerges.

Vital human existence is not disrupted by death. This is discovered through immediate cognition because we directly experience the human ipseity and recognize the permanent nature of its existence. Upon death, we merely shed the corporeal constitution and the concomitant implications of the mortal, biological condition. But we always retain our essential significance.

Clearly, the transformation of the human mentality during our earthly sojourn has enormous constitutional significance. But the metamorphosis of the human soul and our continued progress towards autonomy requires active participation. We do not actually produce the change, but we must position ourselves appropriately through a receptive heart.

One has to realize that the prevailing state of the human soul is such that it is unsuitable for a future of real liberty. But here, in the midst of extraordinary challenges, is the opportune time and place for the cultivation of a mature and healthy disposition. Anxiety, apprehension and defensiveness are the consequence of an uncertain, existential foundation, and a state of emotional anarchy exists beneath a managed facade and superficial comportment that is held in check only because it appears expedient to do so. Therefore, the present condition of the human psyche is hardly suitable or sufficient as a consistent disposition, but it presents an astonishing opportunity.

It is as if our earthly environment were a cocoon in which the transformation of the human soul could potentially occur in a condition proper to an emancipated state. By our direct and consistent will, we enter into a condition of communion with celestial nature through openhearted sincerity. Eventually, the human individual distinction and the metamorphosed soul coincide in an extraordinary integrity of correspondence as a sovereign, autonomous being.

However, the human soul can only reconstruct through active susceptibility, will, and observance, because it is in ourselves that these transformations occur and not merely as an oblique event. Consequently, as with any change of heart, the human soul is the important participant because, even though we cannot transform ourselves, it is the respective individuality that is the subject of the process.

The uncertainly established human soul, defensively preoccupied and anxious of its continuance, is steadily transformed through willingness and concurrence, identifying increasingly with the spirit of the supernal exemplar. Thus, it no longer hinders and pollutes immediate cognition, and the individual is able to engage directly with circumstances without confusion.

Defensiveness is a dire malaise of the human soul that cannot be successfully requited through personal effort. But it is transformed by an immediate, openhearted engagement with a vastly more noble constitution than our own. We discover thereby that our egocentric perspective is superseded by an influence that we refer to as goodwill and integrity. Thus, our little sense of self is transformed and cultivated towards a condition, the nature of which we can scarcely conceive, but we know it will very much resemble the qualitative stature of supernal goodness when it is complete.

At present, the human constitution remains corporeal and mortal because this is the present extent of our development. It is also as far as we are able to proceed without an exhaustive reorientation of the soul. Nevertheless, the Earthly condition has to be temporary, or otherwise it would be an insufferable everlasting torment. Furthermore, it is from the present state that the human soul must be transmuted according to a disposition that is appropriate for a truly meaningful future.

19. Human Destiny

We like to imagine that we are emotionally balanced and indeed, we may appear to be so and, through a combination of benign factors enjoy success and advantage. Some individuals appear to thrive regardless of challenge while others consistently flounder. But, essentially, the human, egocentric mentality must give way to a better and entirely sound nature. The matters under discussion here involve the establishment of a soul-disposition that is appropriate to the furtherance of human development towards sovereign autonomy. From this perspective, the superficial circumstances of our lives remain of lesser significance.

In terms of human advancement towards a destiny of existential and cognitive liberty, an enormously significant dynamic needs to occur within the soul. In light of this, it is pointless to assume that the current emotional status is sufficient because, whether presently it works well for us or not, it is founded upon our own uncertain merit and the accumulated influences that have conditioned our psyche. Born of the past; it remains insufficient to our future condition of liberty. It condemns us to a status quo that is founded upon egotistical narrowness.

However, the process of the qualitative transformation of the soul is made possible only because our own potential maturity is revealed to us directly within the heart. In other words, human destiny is epitomized as an ideal that we experience intimately. In this sense, our own potential full maturity comes back to meet us in order to make possible human development towards existential liberty. Thus, we see that we could never achieve these things without the wisdom and goodwill of the supernal nature within our own hearts.

There is no advantage in being tolerant and making light of the shortcomings and the failings of the psyche because contrition serves us to recognize the redundancy of our familiar mentality. Imagining optimum functionality where, in reality, the human soul exists in a precarious and defensive condition of existential uncertainty hinders our exploration of an approach wherein the human being might become profoundly reconstituted. Thus, we recognize that the pursuit of happiness for itself remains merely a superficial objective. Instead, it is necessary for the human soul to be securely reestablished upon a consistent basis of certainty, with a caliber of character befitting a prospective condition of self-determination and existential liberty.

Immediate cognition through the perspective of the human quintessence reveals the essential condition of things. We directly discover the definitive nature of existence and within our understanding, we progressively build a familiarity with the substantial nature of existence. We come to recognize the tenor of authenticity, and we cannot be deceived because we have discovered the profundity of things through immediate encounter. Thus, we find that the physical appearance and obvious properties of something conceal the intrinsic condition.

In other words, we try conventional beliefs through our familiarity with essential reality, and thereby, compare accepted philosophy against the tenor of our own profound experiences and determine if they ring true.

However, while the application of these things is straightforward, it is not simple. It is not something that can be accomplished without supernal aegis. But, immediately accessible to the human heart is a foundational resource that provides essential assurance from which perspective the human being begins to develop emotional equilibrium. That resource clearly does not originate from our own soul, but it is accessible to us through open-hearted sincerity. Within the human heart, we discover a mainstay, and we cultivate and enhance its significance in order that it may increasingly become the compelling foundation of our feeling nature and ethos. Thus, our emotional nature becomes reestablished upon a condition of soul that is appropriate to a destiny of liberty. Thereupon, the human mentality is no longer capricious and erratic, but it serves the human constitution qualitatively and dimensionally. Amity increasingly becomes the foundation of the soul, and we identify with it as our psychological foundation.

Accustomed and habituated to a mentality oriented towards self-first and survival anxiety we accept the concomitant vicissitudes as commonplace. But a self-centered mentality will inevitably engender friction because each person will promote their own wellbeing. Yet, through open-hearted sincerity, we discover the imminent existence of an opposite foundational premise. It is immediately extant and accessible to us because immanency is the condition of essential existence. That is to say, the superficial appearance of things is spatial, but the intrinsic significance occurs imminently.

Therefore, we immediately experience an intrinsic condition that we can only describe as supernal goodwill.

But it is entirely unlike the egotistical affection that we know. Thus, through immediate communion, we find that it dispels egocentricity entirely from the human psyche and a new foundation of amity and unselfishness becomes established in its stead.

The task is to reestablish the soul upon a secure footing, and we have scant idea what that may be, but, nevertheless, we nurture its development. The choice is always necessarily our own as we turn from our conventional, erratic uncertainty and seek reorientation under the guidance of the supernal exemplar, within an open and sincere human heart.

It is vital that the human soul be actually advanced in this way because a merely ritualistic or intellectual stance is of no value whatsoever when it pertains to intrinsic matters. Therefore, in order that the perspective of the supernal may become our own, we must strive to identify with it. Meanwhile, the conscience readily reveals discrepancies to us, and it is a simple step of willingness to approach the imminent presence within the human heart and allow the supernal to reconstitute our perspective and position the soul on a wise and wholesome footing.

Thus, increasingly, we engage things confidently from an assurance established within the human heart. This disposition develops into a successive ethos to the degree that we sincerely invite its establishment over our familiar, egocentric mentality. Thus, qualitative maturation is increasingly assured through the steady relinquishment of obsolete behaviors and attitudes that work against our further development.

We yearn to live differently from our formerly

impatient, self-defeating, defensive, and uncertain mentality. Consequently, we open the heart and seek a better perspective. Thereby, through attentive willingness, we ensure the establishment of an appropriate point-of-view and subsequent change of heart.

The human mentality at this time is, for the most part, established upon essentially redundant premises and assumptions that are justified only in terms of a superficial, materialistic point of view, but invalid once we glimpse a more profound dimensionality of existence. Within the greater context, populated with essential significances, inherent identity and intrinsic distinction, the conventional materialistic approach and its implications are like a millstone. It is this that makes the commonplace condition of the human soul obsolete because we cannot precede further with a mentality established upon a mistaken way of thinking.

The consequences of a benighted, philosophical point-of-view are blatantly apparent wherever we cast our gaze. Egotism and existential ambivalence are the root of much of the distress and indecency inflicted upon one another and the origin of human discontent. Thereby, the human heart harbors bewilderment and emotional apprehension that possess a destructive momentum.

Once the human soul discovers and directly engages an exemplary disposition through an open and sincere heart, a process of reconstruction commences that establishes a caliber and demeanor that is suitable to a meaningful existence. The soul becomes appropriately transformed to a state of unpretentious maturity that is vital to qualitative progress.

The metamorphosis of the soul is a self-perpetuating dynamic because it begets a profound enthusiasm as we progress. It is further enhanced because we recognize that it is not only a formidable undertaking to attempt to change ourselves, but self-amelioration as an effective and practical approach is impossible without aegis of a vastly higher wisdom than our own. Our task is to be willing to relinquish our old ways and, like a child, allow the supernal nature to replace them with a successive disposition.

20. Soul Metamorphosis

Even with the best of intentions, we cannot possibly transform our own soul through our individual expertise, by intellectual dexterity, or by the power of our will. The dynamic of change is not merely a reorientation or a patch, but a metamorphic transfiguration. Neither is it a matter of finding joy and peace while retaining a moribund mentality. Similarly, it has nothing to do with euphoria, but the new foundation of the soul unfolds systematically and straightforwardly. Accordingly, every step and event of change is authentic and meaningful. In other words, while the heart is the subject of the transformation, the purpose of the metamorphosis of the soul is a profoundly serious and progressive dynamic of maturation.

People sometimes lose themselves in ritualistic excess and hysteria and imagine thereby that they achieve a condition of existential bliss. The conceptual flaw lies in the necessity of constant repetition. However, the metamorphic transformation of the human soul does not require constant reiteration and replication because it is a process of catharsis, dissolution, and the subsequent reconstruction towards a different formation. It is exhilarating because a foundational transformation is taking place that we wholeheartedly welcome, and we earnestly desire to improve. This, therefore, has little to do with the pursuit of superficial benefit.

Indeed, it is a matter of objective. To abandon oneself to excess does not require the assistance of the supernal nature, but it is readily achievable as we now stand. Yet, the qualitative transformation of the human soul from a condition of pettiness and insecurity to certitude and a sound character does not rob us of autonomy, but makes liberty possible.

However, we do not make the transformation happen. Our task is openhearted sincerity and receptivity because, beyond willingness, we have nothing to offer but to allow our psyche to become soundly reestablished by the goodwill of an external agency.

Thus, the metamorphic transformation of the soul is either an authentic occurrence or it does not happen at all. If our approach is superficial or ritualistic, we merely go through the motions without doing the work. It has to be a sincere and actual concurrence, or obviously, it is nothing. That is to say, dispositional rehabilitation requires straightforward, ingenuous attention in order to experience an authentic communion and subsequent meaningful improvement.

In summary, through immediate untrammeled cognition, we discover the authentic and intrinsic condition of things. Nevertheless, in spite of profound insights the soul remains immature. New insights are barely emergent when the old mentality crowds in upon us and obstructs authentic improvement. But the corrective is readily available, but it has to be taken very seriously because what we are embarking upon is nothing less than the establishment of a new disposition. Therefore, as soon as dissonance is evident, we turn within our open and sincere heart and allow our psyche to become impressed by the supernal nature.

Thus, the cognitive liberty of the individual becomes an increasingly feasible concept, established upon a fundamental sense of security that is utterly profound. Thereby, amity supersedes the obsolete, moribund mentality, and the soul becomes reestablished upon the substantial foundation of integrity and goodwill represented by the presence of the archetype of the new human being.

The concurrence and communion of the human soul with the supernal nature ensures that we increase in moral rectitude and respectful dignity because that is the necessary stature of a meaningful human future. Upon our own merit, this is impossible except as a piecemeal gesture. However, what is required is the complete reestablishment of the psyche. Thus, the metamorphosis of the human soul is steadily assured through our own sincerity and willingness, but truly, we would be entirely confounded were it not for the immanent supernal presence to lead us forward appropriately towards maturity and, subsequently, a better future.

Other Books by the Same Author

TOWARDS A MEANINGFUL FUTURE
The Continuum of the Qualitative Expansion of the Soul

THE IMMANENT PRINCIPLE OF INTEGRITY AND GOODWILL
The Integration of the Principle of Virtue within the Human heart

THE EVOLUTIONARY IMPERATIVE OF OUR TIME
The Crucial Establishment of an Inspired Ethos with the Individual, Human Heart, appropriate to a Meaningful Future

RECONCILIATION WITH HUMAN DESTINY
The Surrender of the Heart-of-the-Soul as the Expedient Approach Towards Direct Engagement with the Immanent Exemplar of a Future, Human Disposition

THE QUALITATIVE EVOLUTION OF THE SOUL
The Evolutionary Transformation of the Human Soul Through Openhearted Sincerity Towards Immanent Caritas

THE SUPERNAL ETHOS
Unanimity with the Divine Nature

THE BEGINNING OF WISDOM
Knowledge through Immediate Engagement

UNDER THE AEGIS OF IMMANENT CARITAS
The Reorientation of the Human, Disparate Self-circumscribed Mentality

THE DECEPTION OF MATERIALISTIC WESTERN PHILOSOPHY
An Exploration of the Physically Elusive Volume of Existence

THE MEANINGFUL VOLUME OF EXISTENCE
An Exploration of the Overlooked Intangible Significance of Phenomena

THE OBSOLETE SELF
Individual Uniqueness and Significance beyond Egocentrism

HUMAN SOVEREIGN AUTONOMY
The Discovery of the Human Ipseity and its Establishment as the Essential Authority of the Human Constitution

THE TRANSFORMATION OF THE SOUL
From Self-Centeredness to Sovereign Autonomy

THE IMPLICATION OF HUMAN, INCORPOREAL EXISTENCE
The Overlooked Significance of the Intangible and Qualitative Dimension of Existence

IMMEDIATE EXPERIENTIAL COGNITION
The Inherent Human Capacity of Immediate Engagement

THE HUMAN ESSENTIAL IDENTITY
Direct Experience of Intangible Significance

KNOWLEDGE THROUGH DIRECT COGNITION
The Human Conscious Individuality and Immediately Experienced Reality

www.ingramcontent.com/pod-product-compliance
Lightning Source LLC
Chambersburg PA
CBHW070811100426
42742CB00012B/2328